Remember to Remember:
The Mayan Mysteries

Remember to Remember: The Mayan Mysteries

Carol E. Parrish-Harra Ph. D.

authorHOUSE®

AuthorHouse™
1663 Liberty Drive
Bloomington, IN 47403
www.authorhouse.com
Phone: 1-800-839-8640

First published by AuthorHouse   10/21/2011

ISBN: 978-1-4670-4482-0 (sc)
ISBN: 978-1-4670-4481-3 (ebk)

Library of Congress Control Number: 2011917698

Printed in the United States of America

Any people depicted in stock imagery provided by Thinkstock are models, and such images are being used for illustrative purposes only.
Certain stock imagery © Thinkstock.

This book is printed on acid-free paper.

Dedication

to

Hunbatz Men
Beloved Wisdom-Keeper of the Maya

Who Shares with Many

TABLE OF CONTENTS

Introduction

The Maya say, "Remember to Remember", in the same admonishing manner the Buddhists say, "Right Remembrance", and with the same meaning. "Can you remember who you are"? "Why you are here"? "What is your piece of the plan to fulfill"?

A profound dream captured me in 1985 sending me to seek meaning. I found more and more mystery, and sought to share my discoveries with others. Never having had an interest in North or South American culture, suddenly I was consumed with the mysteries of the Maya. Harmonic Convergence was a big joke to some, and others just thought those confusing new-agers were ridiculous.

On the day of Harmonic Convergence, we awakened before sunlight to salute the sun; we danced, sang, did mudras, and said goodnight to the Sun as he sank over the horizon each evening. We felt like vibrations were changing; perhaps we were.

As a serious pursuer of Ancient Wisdom I would catch a glimpse of one system affirming another and as time passed, the loom on which the ancient truths were woven began to merge. I began to see wholeness in the picture. All were saying the same thing. From psychology, natural scientists, churches and now the ancients, certain truths resonated; even the Gnostics told us of a point in time when we would all awaken.

My incentive for pulling this material together came once I realized how I benefitted by having had a rich exposure to the Maya people, the wisdom-keepers and their culture, I wanted to share the adventure. As I began to glean its perspective and learned its value, I knew others would respect and appreciate the mysteries of the Maya as well. My hoped-for opportunity is to weave my awareness of Ancient Wisdom and these concepts together. I want others to see the richness these concepts have to offer. It is not a separate piece of the puzzle that must stand alone but an integral piece of the whole.

I am grateful to a long line of capable teachers for these insights. I salute them all; the list is too long to name for fear I would leave someone out. I do want to acknowledge those who travelled with me to Maya Land through the years. With Hunbatz Men as leader, we sought together the deeper understanding.

Blessings to all who quest, as we join together in achieving, a more enlightened humanity.

Section I: Introduction to Maya History

The Maya call the Sun, "K'in," the great generator of energy who creates harmony among all the moons and planets of our solar system. Their prayers to "K'in" are to invoke the energy of the creative life force, the transformer of all things, "K'in"—The Sun: the Solar Deity or the Christ, teacher of angels and humanity—serves as the omnipresent, fiery lens through which the universal creative force radiates to the planet Earth, providing for the care and continuance of planetary life. The Maya know this divine force as Hunab K'u, the "One Giver of Movement and Measure."

Everything exists as a result of movement and measure. Hunab K'u, the name for the great God of All, according to the Maya and their calendar, is now reminding us to renew the ceremonial centers of universal wisdom from timeless places of knowledge; voices of the ancients have begun to emanate from rocks, glyphs, and geometry.

The Maya call the planet Earth HU and that the people are called Man and that the sound HU acknowledges the spirit in which we dwell. Much like "in whom we live and move and have our being", HU is also the spirit of the group consciousness known as the collective self or the group soul. Just as Hunbatz acknowledges, the field of consciousness in which we collectively live or create by our expression of life in matter, Rupert Sheldrake called this the morphogenetic field or others the "*L of Life Field*". All indigenous peoples were attuned to the group field of consciousness and used it to sustain themselves. As we speak HU let us remember the human group consciousness which is the "*as below*" or the "*as above, so below*" spiritual principle.

We seek in due time to be a magnificent reflection of the Great Creator as we open ourselves to the Christ Consciousness, called by whatever name, a tradition gives to the Holy that can reflect that high consciousness. The Maya called it "*sun*" and in Christianity it is called "*son*".

We are learning to communicate again with natural forces of creation. To the Maya, knowledge is sacred. Knowledge means "*work with body and spirit*" for each has wisdom to give, says Hunbatz Men, one of the most prominent *Day-Keepers* sharing the tradition today.

He teaches:

For many centuries, initiates of the world traveled to Maya centers from distant countries to study with the Maya solar priests. Here, there once stood Babylonians, Tibetans, Peruvians, and representatives of many cultures, all to partake of this cosmic knowledge." Ancient Maya centers evoked the admiration of many civilizations throughout the world for thousands of years. This is a mind-stretching fact to most who believe modern knowledge is vastly more than what ancient tradition's awareness had to offer.

In *Gateway to Atlantis*, author Andrew Collins, pages 215-216, goes into detail concerning the Feathered Serpent legends.

"The concept of the Feathered Serpent was unquestionably known to the Olmec, for its form has been detected among the formative architecture at La Venta in the province of Tabasco. Monument 19 contains a sculpted image of a rattlesnake bearing an avian beak and a sculpted crest, which scholars consider to be an early re-presentation of Quetzalcoatl.

After the first Quetzalcoatl came many more, for it became a title applied to at least one Toltec lord, who is remembered as CeAcatl Topiltzin Quetzalcoatl. Moreover, the successors of the Toltecs, the priest-kings or Great Speakers of the Aztec Empire, also adopted the title Quetzalcoatl. In this way they saw themselves as lineal descendants of the Feathered Serpent, the reason perhaps why Montezuma was willing to consider Cortes and the Spaniards also were of the 'family of Quetzalcoatl'.

The Feathered Serpent also appears in the mythology of the Quiche of Guatemala. They are one of a whole group of mountain tribes known collectively as the Southern Maya."

Popol Vuh, the most complete Native American spiritual epic we have, could be compared to the *Bhagavad Gita* in importance and content. Veiled in metaphor and allegory, the Maya rendition of the origin of the universe, of gods mating with humans to produce offspring, and an explanation of complex evolutionary cycles, falls to Ethnologist, Raphael Girard, as he offers keys to its understanding.

Girard: *"The beginning of Quiche' (key-shay)-Maya history—coincides with the first races of humans on this continent thousands of years before the Christian era. It follows therefore that; the Popol Vuh is the oldest document known concerning human history, earlier than the Rig-Veda and the Zend-Avesta, until now held to be the most ancient collections of sacred texts."*

Girard published his Spanish version of the *Popol Vuh* in Mexico City in 1948. Only in 1972 did it become available in English. He employs mythology, ethnology, archaeology, and linguistics in his search to become known throughout the world as a most distinguished

"Americanist." In 1977, he was nominated for the Nobel Prize in Literature for his pioneering methods of study of Native American cultures and his monumental writings about their prehistory and history.

The Quiche's creation myths and early history is preserved in the Popol Vuh of Council Book. Here Quetzalcoatl became the "Sovereign Gucamatz" or "quetzal serpent", one of the seven creator-gods who thought to have fashioned the first human beings from a ground mixture of maize.

Dennis Tedlock, the editor of what is arguably the most definitive version of the Popol Vuh, said that these gods were located either "on or in the sea in the primordial world.

Chilam Balam, one of the ancient texts, offers the wisdom of the Maya to those who can decipher such coded material. *Chilam* means "*prophet*" and *Balam* means "*jaguar*". Elders, called "*chacs*" (also the name used for the weather gods, as well as other spirit contacts) help us understand the secrets.

It is said that, then the people forgot their commitment to Hunab K'u, violence fell upon the land, dimming the light of cosmic and universal knowledge. But Maya sages foresaw that with the passage of time, people would return to the land of the Maya, once again to acquire the information from these ageless stones which now vibrate to a new era.

These ancient teachings state the time has come now to *remember* and relearn profound truths with Harmonic Convergence. A Maya emerging today to share the teachings of the Maya is Hunbatz Men. He is called a "*wisdom-keeper*" or "*day-keeper*," the cultural name for their priests and shamans. As a youth, he was trained in the ways of the native people. At about age fifteen he moved to Mexico City to go to high school and college. Though he experienced prejudices toward the indigenous people, he continued his studies at the *Academy of Fine Arts.*

Returning home after four years, he described his struggle to his uncle, his childhood mentor, who advised him his way would be hard; he was to be a teacher and protector of Maya ways. Hunbatz Men is said to be of royal lineage in his particular clan, and this uncle, his mentor, had had spiritual insight as he was an infant that he would come to him when his struggle was intense.

As advised, he dedicated one year exclusively to spiritual study to see if it would engage him. Indeed, he re-discovered peace of mind, health, and joy in the world.

Now he knew he was to share Maya prophecies and teachings. He completed his work at the *Center for Pre-American Culture in Mexico City* and became an author and a highly-sought lecturer on the mysteries of the Maya. He became prominently known through the work of Jose Arguelles, who spread the concept of *Harmonic Convergence* throughout the world. After finding Hunbatz, I located the earliest writing of Jose Arguelles and vigorously pursued to learn what I could.

As Hunbatz was well educated, fluid in Spanish and English, as well as Mayan, he could reach an audience longing to grasp more clearly the teachings he was able to share. The phenomena of Mesoamerica began to attract the attention of the world a decade or two ago. Many buildings, pyramids, and temples are aligned to amplify energy and accent the phenomena of nature and preserve the beliefs that served the Maya.

For a beginning point of each of our journeys into the teachings of Maya, Hunbatz would always take us to Dzibilchaltun, a Cenote, a deep spring at which he would perform a ritual blessing each of us with the waters, and asking us to pray for the well-being of others. This solemn event begins our pilgrimage to learn as much of the Wisdom as we could at the present time.

Receiving the blessing at The Dzibilchaltun Cenote

Another simple piece of advice is given us for important attunement to God's Will. We are to tie about the forehead a blessed strip of fabric kept for this purpose. As we fasten the strip about our head, we ask God to allow us to attune to enter the Great Memory of the Higher Plan.

Hunbatz blessing Mayan treasures for us

In this photo we see Hunbatz blessing two of our Mayan statues to bring home. The Corn Goddess is wooden; her name is IXIM; she abides in my personal collection. The Jade God is called, K'AAX; he resides in the library at Sparrow Hawk Village, Tahlequah, OK.

At both spring and fall equinoxes, a magnificent serpent of light and shadow forms at the *Pyramid of Chechen Itza* (chee-Chi-neet-za) for all to see. This event is called the "*magical descent*" of the Rainbow Feathered Serpent—known as "*Kukulcan*" (koo-kool-kahn) in the Yucatan (yoo-ka-tahn), "*Quetzalcoatl*" (ketzal-kwatl) in the North, and "*Gucamatz*" (goo-ka-mahts) in the South.

Hunbatz says, "Serpent=Snake=Transformation=Ouroborus, and that snake is the name of the healing energy". This pulls many thoughts together and we will see this time and time as we link the Mayan teachings and the Ancient Wisdom together.

Serpents, dragons and snakes have had secret meanings all over the world. The Hindu word "*Naga*", came to mean *initiate.* These were thought to be semi-divine, when they arrived in Hindustan. And the word continues to mean elevated or raised. In a Mayan depiction of energies, the seven stars of the Great Bear are associated with the masculine and the seven stars of the Pleiades are associated with the Lunar or Feminine of Deity. One can easily visualize a ridge pole (The Tree of Life), reminding us of the caduceus.

Quetzalcoatl, as the feathered serpent, found the balance between the masculine and feminine and indeed he can be likened to the androgyny of the alchemist.

Wavy lines of light create the snake, the pure energy of creative intelligence. Hugh crowds gather twice annually to see this holy happening. For one not into Maya belief, this is a phenomena of Light that causes much of the modern world to acknowledge the wisdom of an ancient people who could figure out such a mathematical construction feat.

In "*The Land of White Waters*", Elizabeth Van Buren also states,

> "*the Energies are moving back to the Andes, that great center of the Hierarchy. In (Hu)mans also the right hemisphere is being activated, s/he is regaining the lost powers of his super sensitive mind. The two hemispheres are to function as one again, in harmony. These are the right and left hand of the creator: the LOVE and WILL, the two brothers, the sons of the goddess (Wisdom).*" page 126

Remember, the Aquarius astrological symbol of two waves which represents the awakening of us to the world of vibration or we could say to the etheric reality. In this symbolic system the serpent represents physical world of matter, because it lies close to the Earth using its whole being to inch forward; the feathers are those of the Eagle, because it flies close to Heaven. It represents life alive and well in the non-physical reality. Similarly, the feathers can remind us of the "*thousand-petalled lotus*" of the East. Through symbology, we find suggestions meant to awaken humanity clear and simple.

Wisdom keepers believe a sensitive or dedicated spiritual seeker has only to prostrate him or her-self in a sacred pyramid and the information will begin to flow. The next step is to turn within to reclaim the ancient information impregnated within our essence. Maya believe they will rise again in importance, and humanity will survive the planetary shift from one frequency to another. They have made great efforts to preserve the ancient wisdom over the centuries until this significant time. Now steps have been taken by almost all the native people of North and South America to share their hidden information and assist humanity through the forthcoming difficulties.

The *day-keepers* believe all we need to know is to reconnect to the wisdom of the higher world. It is written and preserved on the stones (hieroglyphs) and by the vibration of the stones. The idea is that as the new Aquarian energy bombards Earth its frequency will vibrate these stones. As the pure one throws her/himself on the plaza or floor in a temple, the vibrations will awaken the energies within the person, and she/he will remember.

Hunbatz says, this is both symbolic and an actuality. Many have already begun the practice of visiting sacred sites to awaken their inner energies and vibrations of a higher sort, hastens the awakening of the kundalini forces and in turn their transformation will be hastened.

Thus we are all instructed to learn to trust our own perceptions. While currently day-keepers continue to travel and teach widely, Hunbatz's major focus is in establishing a spiritual community and cultural center based on ancient Maya principles. Twelve families live at the chosen location with no electricity or modern conveniences. They receive visitors for four months each year. Hunbatz reminds us, modern culture emphasizes the vital importance of money; so often the whole life becomes based on money. Similarly, if the child is taught trees are important, the decisions of life will be made differently.

Mayas relate to a marriage of nature and culture—each community perceiving itself a part of a greater human family that has roles to play in the protection and respect of nature. They perceive that the creation of structures which celebrate the sacred—altars, temples, pyramids, cathedrals—entail the art of infusing the material realm with the spirit reality.

The Maya being closely related to the natives of North America, many of the cultural practices are quite similar. They are found in large numbers and have maintained a quiet underground culture throughout Central America and Yucatan; the Maya overlap Mexico, overflowing into nearby Guatemala, Belize, Honduras and El Salvador.

Maya territory—some 125,000 square miles—encompasses the present day countries of western Honduras, El Salvador, Guatemala, Belize and the Mexican states, as well as the entire Yucatan Peninsula. The southernmost area contains a range of 33 volcanoes. The peninsula begins dry and barren, and becomes a towering rain forest rising out of strangling tropical growth, hot and humid.

In 1992, the entire world watched as Rigoberta Menchu' received the Nobel Peace Prize; she toured many countries and spoke of her people. Her story touched many and provided a new picture of the abuse happening in Guatemala as well as other South American countries.

Everywhere around the world we see new ways, both in feelings and thinking emerging. As old patterns are threatened, a new kind of relationship is being envisioned; one of mutual respect and interdependency. We must ask, "*Is this a reaction to new incoming energies without conscious thought,*" or "*a part of the fulfillment of prophecies of long* ago?" Maya mysteries suggest this is part of the long-awaited "*Age of Illumination,*" or "*Age of Flowers*". Every wisdom system tells of a "*golden age*" when human consciousness will be ready to fulfill its potential.

We ask: *Can humanity find within itself the resilience needed to survive current chaos, creating modern responses to guide us through the changes we face*? As thinking, caring human beings, can we assist in changing a pain-filled world into a renewed *Garden of Eden*, a place of right-relationship, ourselves to one another and to each kingdom of the planet? We will probe what the Maya wisdom tradition has to offer.

In our exploration we will cover:

- First, with the best understanding we can, we will introduce the long hidden tradition from historical data.
- Second, we will get acquainted with a modern wisdom keeper's parables, perspectives and concepts.
- Third, we will familiarize ourselves with the prophecies of the area, most often called Mesoamerica.
- Fourth, we will note the long-concealed secret for which the Maya have awaited announcement.
- Fifth, comparison will be made to other Wisdom traditions.
- Sixth, personal insights gathered from experiences.
- Seventh, suggestions for efforts humanity can make for its well-being.

Beginning in the late 19th century, traditional researchers became very interested in these indigenous people. In beginning to research the Maya, I discovered the work of two of the most respected ethnologists/translators and historical researchers—on this subject were published by the University of Oklahoma. Both Ralph L. Roy's, *Books of Chilam Balam of Chumayel,* and Sir Eric John Eric Thompson, *Maya History and Religion,* dedicated their careers to Mayan studies. Knowing the histories were rapidly disappearing, the University of Oklahoma supported these two historians when there was little interest in Mesoamerican culture.

Ralph L. Roy (1879-1965) was a leading translator of many written works, documents, or parts of a book to be found. In 1933, Carnegie Institution published the first complete translation of a book on *"Chilam Balam,"* with the exception of a somewhat poetic rendering of the same Chumayel by a Yucatan writer and mystic, *Antonia Mediz Bolio.*

It is, however, necessary to emphasize that these are far more than translations. In order to make them, each translator had to steep him or her-self in Maya thought, custom and religion. The struggles are far greater than realized, as the majority of Maya communities have remained isolated until at least the past three decades, particularly in Guatemala. Remember, the less exposed a people are to the outer world, the purer the surviving culture.

Europeans first landed on the shores of Mexico's Yucatan Peninsula early in the 16th century. The great Maya centers were already faded time-honored-relics, worn, overgrown and abandoned. Awe-inspiring remains of more than 60 Maya *"cities"* are simply the most visible and enduring evidence of a civilization spectacular in its achievements. The true dimensions of this unique civilization, however, were lost upon most Spaniards who, in their haste to conquer and convert, failed to comprehend what lay before them. The Mesoamerican tradition built great pyramid structures and placed the temple on the top to be closer to the gods. There seems to be at least 2,000 years in Middle America where pyramid building was an obsession. It is estimated there are at least 25,000 Maya temples located, with only a small number excavated.

Not until the 19th century did the grandeur of Maya culture begin to be explored, awakening the world to this high civilization—similar to the order of Ancient Egypt—that flourished years ago on the American continent.

Similarly, the red and yellow races have preserved explicit prophecies concerning our collective future. Therefore, emissaries from Tibet and the traditional leaders of the native people have undertaken a cultural interchange to clarify them. Mesoamerican prophecy contends that the purpose of the Americas is to unite all cultures and races harmoniously. The Wheel will begin to turn, and the sacred hoop of the Americas will be whole once again.

Hunbatz establishes a tie between Egypt and the Maya through linguistics in his investigations declaring so in his book, *Secrets of Mayan Science/Religion According to High Initiation.* Manetho, the Egyptian priest, historian, and mathematician, maintained that the Maya lived in Atlantis for 13,900 years. Many other historians, priests, and philosophers have attributed to the Maya significant roles in bringing culture to their parts of the world.

Ironically, much of what we know about the Maya and much that we do not know can be laid with equal justice to the same hand in 1562 of a Franciscan missionary named Diego de Landa. Seeking to stamp out heathen practices, ordered the wholesale burning of Maya manuscripts in Mani, a town about 40 miles from Merida. As a result of his zeal, the greatest collection of materials was lost, with remaining manuscripts closely guarded.

De Landa recorded in detail what he could of the Maya—their customs, religious practices, language and system of writing—but he realized his work was inadequate to portray the civilization he was describing. "It may be," he wrote, "that this country holds a secret that up to the present has not been revealed, or which the natives of today cannot tell". He also wrote he had never seen a people so preoccupied with cleanliness. Their religion taught at least one bath a day, which was unheard of by the Spaniards.

It is recorded that Christopher Columbus and his party happened upon a great canopied canoe off the coast of Honduras in 1502 and described it as "as long as a galley" and carrying some 35 men, women, and children. Seated beneath the canopy was the captain or chief who was brought on board Columbus' ship. "They were timid and proper people," the admiral's brother later wrote, "and the women hid their faces behind colorful shawls."

Columbus chose to turn away from the land of the Maya; it would be the Spaniards of 50 years later who would penetrate this mysterious land. After DeLanda's writing and the overthrow of the natives by the Spaniards, the mysteries lay in waiting until the mid-19th century when John Lloyd Stephens, an American lawyer, and the English artist, Frederick Catherwood, ventured into Central America to explore—in the interest of scholarship and art. Truly taken by the profundity of what he found, Stephens did much writing. See: *Incidents of Travel in Central America, Chiapas and Yucatan.*

Stephens grew more and more intrigued by the clouded origins of the ruins he explored. The Maya Golden Age, or Classic Era, as it is called, lasted from at least A.D. 300 to 900, but most Mayanists agree its roots go back to the preceding Olmec civilization, which flourished on the Gulf of Mexico from the years 1200 B.C.—900 A.D., over 2,000 years in duration.

A carving in the Olmec style dated 32 B.C.—with the bar and dot numbering system known to have been used by the Maya—was discovered in 1939. Carbon dating of advanced pyramid construction has placed the dates just before or after A.D. 1. One pyramid, built to a height of more than 60 feet, is typical of the style of encasing an existing structure on the site of another (a layered construction, much like the Russian wooden dolls—one pyramid enclosed within a larger one, and so on, as successive builder chose to expand).

An interesting concept is that the Olmec civilization is believed to be a remnant of the Lemurian civilization, which is believed to have reached a high stature earlier than the Atlantean, with the refined use of the mammalian brain, and did not destroy itself with violence, but ceased to exist by natural causes.

Stories are told saying that Lemurian colonists fleeing destruction in the Pacific left its remnants along the western side of South America to seed the Atlantean civilization that was to come. The symbolic story of *Noah and the Ark* is actually the story of several sub-races out of fourteen sub-races of the Lemurian and Atlantean. Colonists fleeing destruction of their lands provided to successive civilizations all over the world, producing, by constantly changing conditions, the needed stimulation for the ever-evolving human spirit.

Amazing similarities between the civilizations of Maya, Egypt, and India are explained by Maya tradition as carried by colonists from Atlantis fleeing first to the Yucatan (the Americas), then traveling eastward to create the monumental civilizations of Egypt and India. This claim is made frequently as we seriously study the sacred book, *the Popol Vuh*, as well as other materials.

James Churchward used legends of ancient Lemuria to account for these similarities. In his story, Churchward, who had lived in India, said that with the help of an aged priest, in 1868, Churchward deciphered stone tablets written by the Naacals (tribal animal worshippers), and this destroyed land became known as "Mu". The motherland, (the land from which the Naacals came that had existed in the center of the Pacific Ocean), Churchward believed to have been Mu. He learned about the old civilization from the writings left behind on inscribed stones, some weighing 2500+ tons. The priest he met in India transcribed and taught the legends to him.

Churchward calls his stories "*The Remains of Mu*" but claims there are similar stories from many people scattered about the Earth. In his writings, the land of Mu was the center of the Earth's civilization. The tablets tell the story of the great island that trembled and shook like leaves in a tree after a series of earthquakes; then fire from beneath the Earth shot to the heavens, waves flooded the plains, cities were destroyed, and Mu sank in an abyss of fire. He claimed the inhabitants of the west side of South America, the South Pacific islands, and others, are remnants of this sunken society.

The story is told of the time when the waters took away the big Stone of knowledge. Mayan's believe Atlantis will rise again someday. They say the Yucatan peninsula has been under water four times previously. Each time the people simply moved away. They heard the warnings, moved, and returned when the flood waters receded.

We must remember also that Plato writes about Atlantis: Another idea of the old world that bequeathed its inheritance to the modern-world. These ideas fit with the "*worlds*" of the Mesoamerican legends in numerous ways.

The Pre-Hispanic peoples of Mesoamerica recorded the great changes our Mother Earth experienced, too; but they did it with codices. They knew that many of these phenomena were cyclical, because they happened over and over again according to their mathematical cycles. The peoples in Mesoamerica counted these cycles as "*suns*" that are also known as "*solar ages.*"

To be able to understand time, or its cycles, those peoples invented the calendars whose main purpose is to count the cycles of time. Those cycles can be solar, planetary or belonging to any other celestial body. It was then when many peoples on earth created their own calendars. But the most important one is the Calendar of the Sun because it is the main celestial body that rules the cycles in our planet earth.

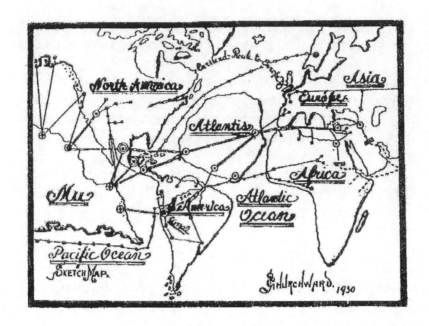

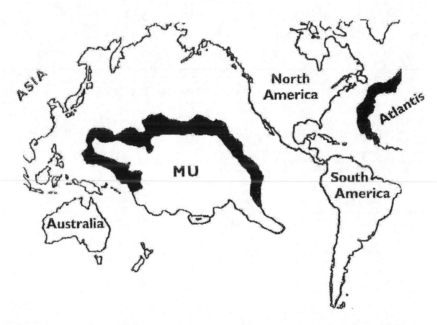

James Churchward shows that two continents once existed and later
disappeared, having been swallowed by the Pacific and Atlantic oceans
These continents were called Mu (or Lemuria) and Atlantis. As one
can see from Churchward's map, the people of Mu were connected to
the Maya, Nahua, Hopi, Inca, Aymara, et al., while at the same time,
all these peoples were connected to Atlantis, which in turn was related
to the Egyptians, Ititians, Babylonians, Hindustanis, et al.

*James Churchward drew a sketch of the two continents (North and South America), with Lemuria
(Mu) and Atlantis penciled in.*

Except perhaps the ancient Egyptians and Babylonians, probably no other people have been so preoccupied with time, as the Maya. They plotted the movements of the planets, Sun and Moon with great accuracy. They tied important events to the movement of cycles. In fact, they knew the Earth was round for centuries, while Europe maintained it was flat. A fascination with time running circles, or cycles, permeates their beliefs. Living rulers repeated the rituals of previous ancestors to maintain cycles of continuity.

Their interest in time caused the Maya to develop mathematics to a degree of sophistication that surpasses the Greeks and Romans. Based on a value of 20, Maya arithmetic used dots and bars and was both fixable and fast in calculating. They were aware of the concept of zero (0), which did not appear in the West until the 12th century. Symbolized by a shell, it was used to signify completion of an arithmetic transaction, as well as the notation for "naught."

From the 8 Calendars of the Maya by Hunbatz Men (page 39), we learn of the seventeen calendars that exist in Mesoamerica. The rest are now lost to us.

A simplified chart of Mayan mathematical configurations.

Mayan Glossary

AHAU – (Ah-ha-oo) – The Mind of Light, The Solar Lord.

AHAU KINES – (Ah-ha-oo Keen-es) – Priests of the Sun, Diviners of Harmony, Solar Lords.

HUNAB KU – (Who-nob-coo) – God, the principle of intelligent energy that pervades the Universe, the Galactic Core.

IN LAK'ECH – (Een-lock-esh) – The principle of Universal Love: "I am another yourself," the Mayan code of Honor.

KIN – The Sun, the chief mediator for Hunab Ku, for our planetary system.

KUXAN SUUM – (Coo-sahn-soo-oom) – Invisible resonant pathways through the galaxy which provide communication: "The Road of the Sky."

MAYA – The Galactic Navigators, the Diviners of Harmony, beings encoded in frequency who travel the Kuxan Suum.

PACAL VOTAN – (Pa-kahl-Vo-tahn) – A Mayan Galactic Master who came to earth in ancient times.

QUETZALCOATL – (Kets-al-co-ah-tul) – Legendary god of the Mayas, the Feathered Serpent, Kukulkan (Coo-cool-con).

TZOLKIN – (Zol-ken) – The Mayan Sacred calendar, the cosmic matrix, the Harmonic Module of Movement (life-giving principle of energy) and Measure (form-giving principle of energy).

ZUVUYA – (Zoo-voo-yah) – The circuit by which all things return to themselves, the Grammar of Harmony, the "Coming from and returning to" the Galactic Core.

UNITS OF MAYAN MEASUREMENT

KIN – 1 day

TUN – 360 Kin (approx. 1 solar year)

KATUN – 20 Tuns (7,200 Kin, or approx. 91+ solar years)

BAKTUN – 20 Katuns (144,000 Kin, or approx. 394+ solar years)

The circle of creation is divided into four equal parts. There are four directions to be realized.

- Balance
- Medicine
- Healing
- God Consciousness

Most of us may think of the Maya as a vanished people, but this is not so. While the culture of the past is almost lost—only day keepers or wisdom keepers being very knowledgeable—presently two million Maya live in their former territories. Hunbatz Men finds it very offensive for anyone to say the Maya were all gone. He defends his people saying they are everywhere unloved, uncared for, with identity and culture destroyed. His efforts are to rebuild our awareness of these who contributed much to our modern way of life.

In the 1840's while political strife was high in Merida, Mexico, the Maya fostered an uprising. Within 15 months, the Maya had gained control of four-fifths of the Yucatan; at planting time, however, they laid down their arms and went home to plant their maize. But the Castle War, as it is called, was far from over; frontier attacks, burnings and looting went on for years. Army after army marched against the Maya, only to be decimated along jungle trails. When 1,000 Yucatan soldiers were killed in battle in 1855, the Mexican government realized they would never subjugate the Maya. Today the Maya still speak their language and remain proud of their lineage.

From the moment of first contact with the outside world on Good Friday, 1519, when Hernando Cortes arrived at Veracruz, Mexico, the white man has recorded his observations of Maya life. The Maya sent scouts to meet the ships, thinking it was Quetzalcoatl returning. The next day the Spaniards went ashore and began the struggle to overpower the people. A chaplain—who took statues of pottery and wood decked with ornaments of low-grade gold from the Maya temple—made the first recording of Maya religion.

We need to remember: Archaeologists study dead cultures, ethnologists study living ones. Ethnologists working in the 1920s and '30s among Maya communities unearthed invaluable remnants of the old religion: ceremonies, beliefs, customs, myths, and so on. Less than 50 years ago, no one dreamed that some Maya communities not only retained the old sacred almanac of 260 days per Maya year, but were still regulating their lives by it.

On each trip to the Yucatan, a visit to a nunnery at Uxmal, we learn here women came to study sacred energies to serve the good of their communities. They worked to bring rain, to insure fertility of the fields, to optimize the male-female gender balance and polarity. They studied the 28-day and 18-year lunar cycles. Regarding sexuality as sacred, the importance of the family unit was taught as the sustainer of social order. The importance of sound, breath, and words was well known. Many temples were built in such a way that when the wind blew, lovely sounds rippled through the temple to make known the presence of gods.

Respect for sexuality resulted in periods of continence, normally reckoned in Maya twenty-day months, or in the highly important 'thirteen-day week" and its multiples; 20 such weeks represent the 13:20 vibration. Men and women slept separately in preparation for important ceremonies. Failure to observe continence before a ceremony was regarded as dangerous to both the individual and to the community throughout the Maya area.

Addressing some of the challenges we encounter translating Maya hieroglyphs into our concepts, Hunbatz explains: The Maya have only one word for science and religion. Religion is the science of living in harmony, or in alignment. Similarly, space and spirit are the same word. If you are in spirit, you are in space. This does not mean "out in space", but focused in your space body, your non-physical body.

The difficulty exists when the teachings refer to an alignment with planetary influences of galactic importance, or when there is a reference to the influence of an ancestor in another dimension (spirit) and the translator does not know which is meant since the term can be used either way.

Obedience to "The Word" is significant in each religious or legal system and was from the beginning, language was a privilege of the Maya, for in their earliest worlds there was no language, only instinct. As so many other ancient cultures they developed a system of hieroglyphs like the Egyptians or Cuneiforms of the Sumerian's. An appreciation of language is gradually gained even as we today are attempting to appreciate the communication tools from culture to culture.

Many such discoveries are still being made because Maya culture did not die with the Spanish conquests; this ultraconservative system went underground to save itself and to preserve its heritage. Written in native languages and some Spanish, a wealth of detail on religion, history and myth remains in several sources, such as the books, *Chilam Balam* of the Yucatan area and the *Popol Vuh*, considered the Mayan Bible.

The Spanish Conquest was designed to devastate the Maya. As old religion was uprooted, the Maya were gathered into towns to be instructed in Christianity and kept under surveillance, less they slip back into heathenism. They were placed under the domination of the white race, which neither knew nor cared about the Mayan ways.

After the Spaniards' arrival, great sweeps of the rain forests were left almost uninhabited because of the spread of newly introduced diseases—particularly malaria, yellow fever, smallpox, influenza and syphilis.

> "*It is estimated that as many as 90 percent of the native population of the Americas died of disease or violence in the first century of the Conquest, as many as 50 million people.*"—*Legacy,* 1992, Maryland Public Television.

However, little changed for the peasant who had been forced to build temples and pyramids to the old gods, and then they found themselves slaving for foreigners. Now they toiled at pulling them down to erect on their foundations Christian churches of such dimensions as to shock Saint Francis. All of this was not fatal to the Maya culture; friars were too few to keep strict control over their flocks and with little understanding of the old ways, they were unaware of what was happening at the ceremonies in forest clearings.

The "*ceremonial center*" pattern of Maya communities can be observed most easily today in the uplands of Guatemala and Yucatan. In the study of the Maya culture, symbols (and myths) reveal secrets stored in design; symbols and customs exist tucked away in the dark cupboard of the mind, from whence they will tumble, like building blocks, when needed. A fresh interpretation of history is developing as the consciousness of the new era demonstrates respectful interest in ancient ways.

There were, in fact, two Maya religions—one of the ruling class, the other of the peasant. We study the religion of the peasant today for it is the one of which more ancient remnants have survived, at least partially intact. In contrast, beliefs and practices of the ruling class died when their sons were forced to be educated under Franciscan priests who made themselves responsible for the education of the sons of nobility and priesthood. Thus, the *mission-educated* covered the old religion with a veneer of Spanish religion. The Maya faith of the ruling class version disappeared in a few generations.

Mayan hieroglyphs were too complicated to translate before the development of sophisticated computers. Only with our technological progress/evolution could we begin to translate the possible meanings of Mayan numerical codes and hieroglyphics or break through to any understanding of their complex calendars.

We find two distinct levels of understanding among the historical people. The first, the classic wisdom, was for the priests, the mathematicians, the calendar makers, and the wisdom (or day) keepers. The land keepers of the second group were the nature people, simple peasants who protected the body of Mother Earth who had offered herself to the seeds and souls that wanted to come here for a place in which to grow, to evolve, and to reach illumination.

Once precise calculations to put our planet into place for Galactic alignment, were established these mathematicians, priests and calendar makers disappeared. Departing in about, 830AD, their wisdom left behind in myths and prophesies; the concluding effects to be fulfilled according to the evolution of the human: after, 2011 or 2012AD, there should be a rapid unfolding of new planetary civilization.

Today's interest in things Mayan naturally spans at least 2,000 years. Thus until this century, the language and culture have survived. But now, as the process of integration accelerates, the red (race) ways and red speech continue to be modern victims. Surviving customs are melting away like snow in the sunshine. Nevertheless, principal teachings and wisdom-keepers remain, and to them we look for information.

As with other sacred writings that offer us a picture of a peaceful era ahead, the Maya say the *future* is to bring a millennium of perfect peace for those who have come to know and use their talents to aid the planetary family—male and female—from every race and walk of life. They live in every location upon the Earth Mother and have one common characteristic: their ability to live in peace with who they are, with each other, and with all our relations. They don't have to be chiefs; they do not want to leave the Earth for another home.

In his book, *Maya History and Religion* (1970), p. 164), historical sociologist, Eric Thompson, says little understanding exists in the modern renewal of Maya culture of the state religion of Ceremonial Centers where the priest, ornately decorated, performed his rites atop a high pyramid far above the crowd of peasants gathered in the court below.

With the collapse of these centers and the massacre and expulsion of nobles and priests, only the folk religion remained, with its dedication to the gods of the soil, the hunt, and of the village. The awakening world is now seeking the wisdom hidden in the teachings of indigenous people to see if we can re-discover a way of life, peaceful and serene.

The classic high priest's main functions were to teach candidates for priesthood hieroglyphic writing, calendar computation, rituals, divination, and the art of prophecy; the priesthood was passed down to the nearest male relative.

Minor priests, or prayer-makers, practice cures and divination in present-day Yucatan, as well as taking charge of community rites in connection with fields and forest. In the Guatemalan highland the shaman, or prayer-maker, functions in a similar way and is, so to speak, a member of the clerical guild. In the Yucatan the wisdom or day-keeper, as they like to be called, remains as a self-employed professional.

Since I am not planning on being so technical as some about "time" as some others, I want to offer a simple perspective of the issue as I understand it. There is a theory of a natural advancement in human consciousness, both singularly and collectively. This natural expansion of consciousness is achieved by each as they learn to harmonize with other forces of nature in the world around them. In other words, there is a "gear" turning that is our natural speed; there is also nature's natural "gear". They work like the back of the old-style watch. The gears support each other; so many turns of one make the other advance as well.

Using this theory, there are planes of consciousness naturally in place in our universe. As we achieve a level of understanding, we progress toward the next plane. The human body is nature's calculator or basic numbering system. Since each person has ten fingers and ten toes, each one is already set for a 20-digit gear; with each of us having 13 major joints in our body. The human being is naturally operating on a 13:20 Universal Timing frequency, so explains this system.

Our artificial system created a 10-digit system because it was easy, but it is not in keeping with the laws of nature, so says Arguelles—in thousands of words. He is genius in his words but hard to follow. Using the simple approach of the body as a key, he suggests the expansion of consciousness will move into higher dimensions as we adjust to the natural rhythm of the Universe.

There are numerous examples in his work, but think only in a simple way. Each of us are exploring our reality—becoming conscious—with our ten fingers and toes (20 digits) and learning in regard to the solar system which operates on a 13 frequency. There are twelve constellations circling our sun making 13-players in our cosmic game. We have to gear up our 20-digit system (*fingers and toes*) to merge in order to operate in a 13-player game. This is called the 13:20 Universal Timing Frequency.

In its design, the Thirteen Moon 28-Day Calendar represents a perfect harmony of time. It aligns us with the human female "Moon" or biological cycle of 28 perfect days, thirteen times a year. Each of the thirteen perfect moons has a power, action and quality that form an annual path for the return of the collective Mind, Will, and Spirit. Each day has a unique energy, guiding power, and purpose that tune us in to the flow of the universe. Based on the Tzolk'in, or Sacred Calendar of the indigenous Maya, this accurate timing device stimulates waking up and remembering again our journey as our family, one species with one origin and destiny.

The adoption of the Thirteen Moon Calendar requires that we step forward trusting in others and the goodness of life. Much of the acquisition of money on our planet has involved completion, based on materialistic thought forms and fear that there is not enough to go around. The freewill choice to adopt the calendar of thirteen moons helps to dissolve this old way of thinking. The calendar becomes our template for peace and true time. It leads us to Universal Telepathy, where everyone feels free to help everyone else through co-operation, teamwork, and mutual support. As we tune in to our true timing frequency, we advance towards this long-awaited Oneness of Spirit. Others will follow our path of Light and Love as we raise our frequency from 12:60 to 13:20.

To restore the dominion of natural time, human beings will need to raise their frequency. When we choose to leave behind the artificial time of 12:60 (12 month calendar, 60 minute hour), and focus on the natural power of moon time, we use our free-will to restore humanity's lost sense of Oneness. From the Tzolk'in, template of galactic time, 13:20 refers to the thirteen tones of creation, combines with the twenty solar tribes of humanity, countable on our body's fingers and toes.

Chris and Linda Lucz-Hatifeld, Blue Spectral Eagle and Blue Self-Existing Monkey . . . From Wacah Cahn Fall 1995

Our real work is to begin to operate in harmony with the heavens, or the frequency of the heavens. We are in the process of learning to employ our physical vehicles in harmony with the higher world. This is placing our actions—karma translates as action—in harmony with higher will. Nothing new here, but it is being said in new terms to us who have been geared to a 24:10 system, that works fine on a 3-dimensional reality.

But as our consciousness or even all consciousness (nature) around us is evolving toward a fourth dimensional reality; it no longer works and all breaks down. This is the struggle between the world of materialism and the world of spirituality. At the fourth dimension we view each other as spiritual beings struggling—or pulled by forces of nature—to find their way to the Oneness. The Maya and their great leaders, who can explain better than I, would say this is the action we are attempting as we travel toward 2013.

Since the year 2013 will arrive shortly after Winter Solstice 2012, I think it should be a very different year for us and we should be ready to live much less "materialistically", and much more "spiritually"—not knowing exactly what the Universe is going to ask of us.

To get an idea of the stories in the *Popol Vuh*, knowing it serves as religious law, and/or provides as articles of faith given to humanity by the Mayan deity, *Hunab K'u*. His son, *Hunab P'u*—the civilizing hero of the Maya culture—is a redemptor-god and Son of the Supreme Being. Like all great religious founders, he is born immaculately and sacrifices himself for humanity many centuries before Christ Jesus comes. Accordingly, Hunab P'u proclaimed the soul's immortality before Plato taught.

Hunab P'u (male) and *Ixbalamque* (eesh-ba-lom-kay) (female), male and female twins, were born at dawn on winter solstice, the story goes. They transform themselves into "*human beings,*" taking on the experience of human life to establish patterns of conduct. He is often regarded as the "*young Maize god*" and is sometimes (often) compared to *Osiris*. She is considered the *new moon-goddess* and is inseparable from the growth of maize. The two remind us of Hindu "*gods and goddesses*" or consorts—even as Jesus and Mary are Divine male and female incarnating to do a work together. Later this story changes to be two male twins, but originally it was male and female. In later stories of the twin boys we can think of *Humanity and its Collective Shadow*.

Hunab P'u establishes rules for worship, cultivation of fields, and lays down astronomical rituals and *time-reckoning* procedures inseparable from those rules. He provides an understanding of natural law and ethics, as well as religious morality based on the conservation of individual, family, and society. He represents the ideal human type in its earlier development.

Before we completely leave the subject, it was helpful to me to know that Pierre Teihard de Cardin struggled with the same issue. I had no idea, so I am going to quote one paragraph of his thinking and leave it to you to mull over from there.

> "*The first stage was the elaboration of lower organisms, up to and including man, but the use and irrational combination of elementary sources of energy received or released by the planet. The second stage is the super-evolution of man, individually and collectively, by the use*

of refined forms of energy scientifically harnessed and applied in the bosom of the Noosephere, thanks to the coordinated efforts of all men working reflectively and unanimously upon themselves . . . In becoming planetized, humanity is acquiring new physical powers that will enable it to super-organize matter. And, even more important, is it not possible that by the direct converging of its members, it will be able, as though by resonance, to release psychic powers whose existence is still unsuspected?" Pierre Teihard de Cardin

The identification of telepathy with the velocity of time emphatically underscores de Chardin's final point . . . connected by a telepathic network that greatly diminishes reliance on much of the technology that characterizes the Technosphere*—the mid-world, (my word, not his).

*TIME & THE TECHNOSPHERE, Jose Arguelles, Page L8

My simple drawing of all this complicated language goes back to wisdom teachings and the idea of three worlds offered by major concepts. Let us look at this:

Various Worlds We Live Within

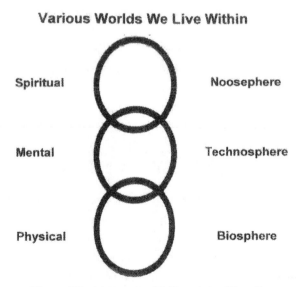

Spiritual		Noosephere
Mental		Technosphere
Physical		Biosphere

Three Worlds as per Teilhard de Chardin

Since humanity is the only "consciousness" that deviates from a pattern of set behavior, (it has been willed as free will from the Creator) it is up to the collective of humanity to grow in consciousness in such a way that it decides it will work harmoniously with higher will, so as to move to the Noosephere or to the world of higher dimension. It is a choice, but humanity has hemmed itself in by reckless disregard of higher will to the tests of this time in history. This is, in fact, the message of the Maya and their teachings are to assist a pressured humanity to coordinate the laws of nature with the laws of higher planes, to get us ready for the shift into the higher frequencies.

The Maya religion, one of salvation, has as its ultimate goal the development of inner tranquility of soul within a harmonious social order. Understanding moves humanity from *holy concepts* to the superimposed planes of heaven and earth. This cosmic quadrangle—determined by four celestial points—is divided into four equal parts by the astronomical cross: solstices and equinoxes.

On this playing field we find what we know now as the *ball game* can be traced to the Maya as a sacred game. The story of The Sacred ball game is preserved for us as a legend picked up in Maya.

> *The favorite game of Middle America before the Spanish conquest was a curious, and violent, cross between soccer and volleyball. It was more than a game, as it had religious meaning and was a vital part of community rituals, often leading to sacrifice and death. The ball game, as best it is known, was first played by the Olmecs by 400BC, and over the centuries spread both north and south.*
>
> *In Mexico City there are several massive I-shapped courts with stone rings and exaggerated end pieces where the game was played. There it evolved uniquely according to scholarly interpretations of a fresco and a number of stone post assemblages, it differed from other versions. Sticks were used, swung perhaps as in ice hockey today; the game was played in a relatively informal area; and third, vertical stone posts seem to function as special goal posts.*
>
> *Nevertheless, it is the Aztec version that is best known today because more of their ball courts have survived. Also, both Aztec and Spanish historians have left accounts of their games.*
>
> *In the game, two teams face each other over a line drawn across the center of the court between two giant side walls. Their aim is to knock a heavy rubber ball into their opponent's end of the court . . . like many sports today. The players were only allowed to bounce the ball off the walls, and to hit it with their hips, knees, or elbows. Teams could win a game outright by knocking the ball through either of two stone rings that jutted out from midpoint of each side wall. Rings were 20 ft. or more above the court, and just big enough for the ball, so goals were uncommon. A player who scored was allowed to confiscate the clothes and possessions of any spectators he could catch.*
>
> *Players wore padded knee-caps, leather aprons, face-masks to protect themselves from the flying ball, and gloves to protect their hands from the stony ground when they fell. Injuries were common and sometimes fatal.*
>
> *The game was so popular that goods were wagered on the results. In the 15th century the records tell of an Aztec emperor playing against the ruler*

of a neighboring city, bet the market-place of Mexico City against one of the ruler's gardens, and lost.

Wherever the ball game was played, it had, besides the popular appeal, ritual importance. Ball courts were always east-west or north-south, and each part of the game had its own significance. The court represented heavens, the rings symbolized sunset and sunrise or the equinoxes, and the movement of the ball represented the path of the sun, moon, or stars, depending on the belief of that area. Some matches even ended with the ritual sacrifice of the losers.

The game was used for divination among the Aztecs—as when Montezuma played against the lord of the nearby city to test the truth of a prophecy that strangers would come to rule Mexico City, then Tenochtitlan. The legend records that Montezuma won the first few games in the series, but was then defeated—and it was not long afterwards that Cortes landed to begin his conquest of Mexico.

Tales of the game are plentiful. Importance is given to special periods of the calendar, recalling the relationship of the physical world to the movement of heavenly bodies. The game was utilized also as a means of settling disputes in the manner of jousts and tournaments.

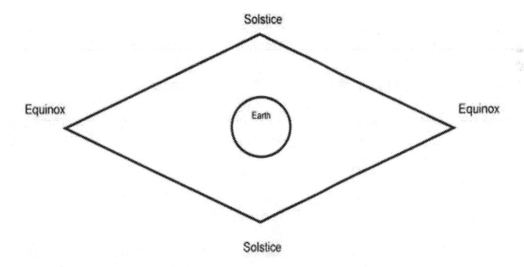

A diamond shape is the ballpark with the four Chacs stand at the points of Solstice and Equinox, they hold a creative moment and flash of light produces the Earth.

The Creation Story as it relates to the importance of the ball game and the chacs: The chacs (Lords of weather; earth, fire, wind and rain) simultaneously gave a command, each squared off at an angle of the heavens. Earth is formed by the four gods (think of these as the Ritualistic Archangels of the solstices and equinoxes) holding a single thought and directing their energies to a single point in the center.

Here we have the *Creation moment,* and a Divine spark in the center spews and sparks to form Planet Earth.

The Indian measured heaven and earth, established points, squared the universe, and built all models of territory, village, field, altar, house and plaza by this concept. The four directions were indicated by landmarks, markers and principal colors: East—red (blood), North—white (Moon), West—black (wisdom), and South—yellow (Sun).

Now all the energies of earth, water, fire, and air blend in the formation of the planet. As it rounds the corner of time, it spirals upward refining each original ingredient; thus, our planet evolves upward thru the planes on a spiral from materialism to the higher worlds. The consciousness of humanity and the forms of the lower world are evolving as they spiral upward—frequency and dimension to dimension.

Quetzalcoatl uses the energy of the galaxy as he presides over the region of the Earth. It is often shown as a flat plain or level a well-known example is the sacred ball diamond. Quetzalcoatl carries the plane marked with planetary symbols to represent the many influences he distributes.

Galaxy is a respectful title for the great Cosmic Egg from which life as we know it descends. G is the name of the "Egg" whenever it is presented. Pronounced "ga", it identifies itself as the Great Egg wherein all life exists.

Ancient Maya texts describe the first inhabitants of the Yucatan as arriving by boat from the East after a freak flood. It claims the familiar Maya profile as characteristic of the people who traveled to the Yucatan from Atlantis following that continent's submergence.

Ancient wisdom offers the idea that the World Tree appears everywhere. The massive, towering *Ceiba tree* represents the *sacred Tree of Life or World Tree of the Mesoamerica tradition,* and is said to mark the *exact center of the world*. Teachings say the tree represents the links between levels of the Cosmos; its roots descend into the underworld, its trunk stands in the middle world, and its branches reach high into the heavens, or upper world. Because of its critical role in the atmospheric rain cycle, the tree is revered as the sustainer of life. The Maya say: *"From this Tree the first human emerged . . . with the death of the last tree comes the death of the last human."*

As a shaman in his tradition, Hunbatz Men says, *"In Mayan there is no separate image for God; it is a pure concept; Hunab K'u, the Giver of Movement and Measure, is in everything."*

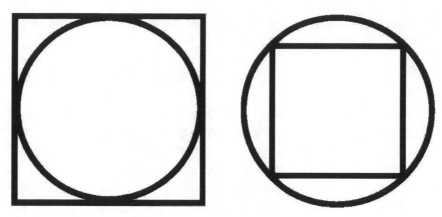

Hunab K'u: *The symbol of movement and measure*

Viewing the movement of all things in the Cosmos as hooked to time and/or frequencies, the Maya believe that to comprehend time and movement is to know God and the Galactic Mind. As accomplished navigators, familiar with plane and spherical trigonometry, they computed the size of the world, estimated the distance from pole to pole and calculated the length of meridians. Their buildings were designed to embody concepts of the physical and spiritual relationship to the Cosmos. Certain hieroglyphic inscriptions record events that occurred some 400,000,000 (400 million) years ago. Hunbatz Men says this number is symbolic of their understanding of the importance of 20x20. It is both symbolic and coded, like a Kabalistic blind.

Hunbatz claims his spiritual duty is to "*wake people up to the energy of the Solar Deity" (the Sun,) for High Knowledge is coming, we must prepare to receive it.*" Modern Maya believe the time is now to work with others to reopen the schools of ancient knowledge and to teach their ways once again. We are to learn what each of the sacred centers of the world offers so we may become the kind of human beings needed for the *new solar age.*

The entrance into the new Itza (eet-sa) age is analogous to the Age of Aquarius, using the calculations of Harmonic Convergence we will have fully entered the new age by 2013. We will be out of the 25 years marked by Harmonic Convergence (transition period) by then. This exactness differs from many other traditions. It is now time to awaken to the deeper part of our being, regaining the information imprinted in the spiral of our DNA.

For a better understanding, we need to remember as we proceed into a new sign, the Greater Zodiac moves counterclockwise to our planetary system. We depart the age of Pisces and back into 30-degrees Aquarius. The assigned Sabian symbol addresses' the topic, as:

> "*Deeply rooted in the past of a very ancient culture; a spiritual brotherhood in which many individual minds are merged into the glowing light of a unanimous consciousness is revealed to one who has emerged successfully from metamorphosis*". (The keynote: *the ability for the person*

with an open mind and a deep feeling for self-transcendence to come in contact with higher forms of existence).

Dane Rudhyar, An Astrological Mandala

Back to our story: In 1519, 13 heavens (full title "Heart of Heaven"), the positive, good times for the culture came to an end with the arrival of the Spaniards; the Maya knew they were entering a period of a dark cycle, moving into the World of the Nine Lords of Darkness, or the Nine Hells. Certain families (true also among other Native American groups) were entrusted with sacred information and the responsibility to keep it secret. Information was taught only to a chosen few and it was to be retained orally to keep it out of the reach of others.

The *Popol Vuh* sheds light on the whole outreach of Native American spiritual thought. This demonstrates at the heart of Maya religion and custom there is a sophisticated spiritual philosophy, corresponding not only to ancient Mexican creation mythology, but also to the perennial wisdom of many other ancient civilizations. This text is indeed a mystery document; a great deal of wisdom emanates from it. The more we see the more is revealed and comprehended.

This Mesoamerican world of metaphysical complexity is made up of worlds and planes by the emanation of seven-fold creative forces that continue to inspire its creation. Here we are introduced to *four creative cycles*, sometimes called, *"worlds,"* each with its respective humanity in relationship to the whole of humankind—not just Maya. As we enter the new era, we are taught it is time for the people of all four directions of the planet to come together for the beginning of a new era of multicolored beings; the *Rainbow People*, or *Rainbow Tribe.*

We are wise to remember the Root Race tradition of the Theosophical teachings and the coming of the *Sixth Root Race*, please, by C. W. Leadbeater, Theosophical Press.

Now, in this 1987-2012 era, in preparation for this new world, according to Maya thought, humankind has been achieving conscious spiritual linkage through the mediation of the *god-man,* (we could also say *Adam Kadmon* or the *Christ),* and return to high consciousness after a time of having *"lost"* our divine connection. We can compare this idea to *"Christ's departure and return"* to modern-day humanity after the work of the *Holy Spirit* (the raising of our vibration) assists us to know our Oneness.

Regarding the second coming, we recall John 14:3, *"And if I go and prepare a place for you, I will come again and receive unto myself: that where I am ye may be also."* Or, Ephesians 4:13 *"till we become one and in the knowledge of the Son of God, and become a perfect(ed) man, according to the measure of the stature of the fullness of Christ"* . . . In <u>Romans 12:5,</u>

So we, [being] many are one body in Christ, and every One members One of another."

In order to achieve this contact, the esoteric Maya doctrine explains the individual cannot realize the perfect state of "*True Man*" (we could say *Mystical Christ*) or "*Hunab Pu*", except when the whole community attains that divine perfection. Here is found an unmistaken reference to the doctrine of oneness, compassion, its path, and the hierarchy which sustains it. This parallels with the message of Christ Jesus and his words of "*love thy neighbor*" and "*So we, being many, are one body in Christ.*"

In *Esoteric Christianity* we would say, '*able to find answers in the heart*' and '*have knowledge that humankind is the true son of the Creator*' and '*become "perfect(ed)". We are to become aware of the Christ within*" or *we cannot become 'One', and we each are to be such*'.

Here in the Mayan teaching, again, we find the emphasis on the oneness of humanity—we are each a part; or as a Kabalist, we recall Adam Kadmon—the wholeness of humanity is united in its spiritual nature. Again and again we get this idea of its divine Oneness; we find it everywhere.

Four hundred years ago a *Quiche'* (key-shay) wise man wrote down the *Popol Vuh* in his own language, but with roman letters. Early in the 18th century (1701-1703), Father Francisco Ximenez discovered the *Popol Vuh* and translated it to Spanish. The text itself has no division into chapters or areas, but is one continuous narrative from beginning to end.

Typical of Quiche'-Maya mindset, this reflects the Maya's lack of seeing life in broken segments, seeing all life as archetypal—therefore, life has no break, or never-to-be-broken, no separation from Cosmic order, but as one continuous past, present, and future—its myths are foundation stones for the collective evolving consciousness.

In teaching these concepts, Hunbatz suggests we look around, and you will find you cannot see yourself as a young child lying over there, a teenager lying elsewhere, and young adult here at your feet. You are not separated into parts and neither is your being—essence—separated into parts. You are all one—within and without—a combination of all parts to make a whole. You have grown your infant consciousness into an older understanding, and all humanity is doing likewise, because we think we are in parts; we error.

Now, let us look at how these ideas can be ordered. To the Maya, we live in the ending of the fourth (this is in disagreement in various traditions) world.

> "*Regarding the World Age Cycle we are closing in 2012 and the new World Age cycle to dawn, there are varying cosmologies as to whether we are closing the Fifth World and entering the Sixth, or closing the Fourth World and entering the Fifth. For example, In the perspective of the living Maya timekeepers of Guatemala, calendrically speaking, each element has a 5,125 year cycle. They teach that we have been through fire, air and water already. The next cycle (beginning Dec.21, 2012) will be*

ether-the Fifth Age-The Age of Center. Likewise, the Hopi teach we are closing the Fourth World of Destruction, and preparing to begin the Fifth World of Peace. Regardless of the title, what is clear is that we are poised on the brink of a World Age Rebirth. www.13moons.com *2005 SkyTime 800-596-0835*

The previous ages are nonexistent but have been taken apart, and the ingredients transformed into the present existing reality. (Example: An adult is the transformed child; the child isn't lying around discarded somewhere.) The worlds are divided from one another by a period of destructive cataclysms that annihilates the previous civilization—the infrastructure. One can no longer look at it because it ceases to exist, but one can remember, integrate lessons learned, and rebuild on its knowledge.

Preceding worlds belong to pre-history, but in Maya thinking, even though disintegrated, their remnant thoughts/knowledge hold the causes of the foundation of the new world. In reality the past is never gone; it is again incorporated into today. We might see these as *"influences"* carried forward in the collective unconscious, or even that our collective karma provides each world with its new learning experience.

Remember the various people or tribes in both North and South America differ in the number of preceding ages that have existed. Theosophical teachings will use the idea that there have been previous root races; now we are nearing the time of the next root race, the sixth called Aurorean. Afterwards, a seventh root race will be created to complete humanity's great journey. We can call these *"waves of consciousness,"* or we can think of them as *root races* or *worlds* as has been the way some others have identified them.

ROOT RACE

In esoteric terminology seven stages of humanity , a series of GROUP MINDS, develop during the cycle of planetary existence. As Earth's humanity passes through these seven root races, the human life stream evolves. These progressive epochs of dominant cultural complexes, or peoples, are centered in geographic areas where the stream of divine sparks converges into expression: a root race.

According to esoteric tradition, the seven primary groups, in order, are: Adamic, Hyperborean (the first two groups, or races, did not take physical form), Lemurian, Atlantean, Aryan – the American-European group mind is the fifth SUB-RACE, or the fifth part of the fifth root race in esoteric determination. Two are yet to emerge (the sixth has been named Aurorean; the seventh is yet unnamed).

Each root race contains seven sub-races, which are like waves coming upon a shore, each evolving toward the goal of the root race in its cycle. Divided into seven sub-periods, or sub-races, each root race attains to a climax of achievement about its midpoint, the 4th sub-race

Here a racial cataclysm begins. Both a new race and the next sub-race are born of the fifth sub-race of the root race as it declines. The new root race then evolves parallel to the latter half of the preceding mother race. The sixth and seventh sub-races continue to perfect the goal of the root race. The intent of the term specifies humanity as a race of peoples evolving and achieving specific evolutionary purposes for the whole of humanity, not in the sense of distinct ethnicities within the whole.

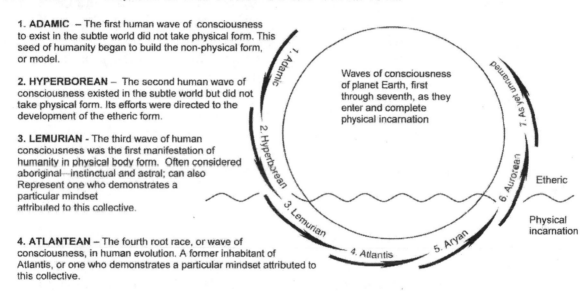

1. ADAMIC – The first human wave of consciousness to exist in the subtle world did not take physical form. This seed of humanity began to build the non-physical form, or model.

2. HYPERBOREAN – The second human wave of consciousness existed in the subtle world but did not take physical form. Its efforts were directed to the development of the etheric form.

3. LEMURIAN - The third wave of human consciousness was the first manifestation of humanity in physical body form. Often considered aboriginal—instinctual and astral; can also Represent one who demonstrates a particular mindset attributed to this collective.

4. ATLANTEAN – The fourth root race, or wave of consciousness, in human evolution. A former inhabitant of Atlantis, or one who demonstrates a particular mindset attributed to this collective.

5. ARYAN – The fifth wave of consciousness in human evolution, as determined in esotericism; from *Aryavarta* (thus "Aryan") ancient name of north-central India. The Indo-European-American group mind is its fifth sub-race.

6. AUROREAN – The sixth wave of consciousness said to be appearing about A.D. 2400 in southern California and at the edge of Mexico. The teachings say the current fifth sub-race of the fifth root race will give birth to this sixth. The contributions of the Slavic people are considered significant to this emerging next wave of consciousness, yet it will be a mixture of all ethnicities.

7. SEVENTH ROOT RACE – Too far in the future, approximately 500,000 years, to have been named as yet. It is believed by most to be of a much subtler form, not in physical bodies such as we know now—perhaps etheric in nature, with a different means of reproduction.

Carol E. Parrish – Harra. *The New Dictionary of Spiritual Thought*. Oklahoma: Sparrow Hawk Press, 2002

Root Race Information and drawing *from The New Dictionary of Spiritual Thought by Carol E. Parrish-Harra*

Present day culture then is a product of all these levels of history. The Maya believe the greater contribution of history is that it propels the new world into a higher frequency. The cultural advance of each cycle is directly proportionate to the wise use and comprehension of the enduring wisdom gleaned from the previous ages. Respect for the past is needed to be understood today. The Maya express this as the course of events in which the present world had its beginning or origins. Thus, time weaves the future out of the past. We are now completing the work of the world in transition, and the collective is purifying the consciousness of all so we can begin the next world without such struggles as we have had regarding *separation* and *materialism*.

History perceived in this way creates a picture of *"First World Human, Second World Human, Third World Human"*, and *"Fourth World Human"* etc. The family provides the picture of a particular civilization, and pictures—iconography—preserves as *"right pictures"* to help future people remember. For the Maya, a belief in causal connections continuing its outworking is much like our understanding of *seeds of karma* still at work.

Teaching myths, stories or parables are used to explain many practices and ideas in all traditions. To live and act in accordance with mythical patterns is the constant aspiration of the *Quiche' Maya*. To establish harmony between *"now"* (life) and *"then"* (the myth), ceremonies are used to remind—call into our inner mind, not necessarily for discussion, but to some level of self; even the cells remember.

The past is ever present; but reliving it (through ritual or dance) stirs the deeper memory and helps one attune to his or her inner knowledge. Native elders are trained to remember; unlettered to us, they carry on the great oral tradition. Similarly, the Hindu people handed down the texts of the *Vedas* orally and with age-old accuracy of at least the last 2,000 years.

Although the culture may seem to be broken to us, the *Maya-of-today* lives in the mythological fourth world-*of-a—sacred-space and time (compared to the aborigines living in dream time)*. A sense of security is achieved through this spiritual connection. The *Popol Vuh* then is the study of fundamental questions and problems, as well as human life and destiny throughout humanity's entire evolution. It gives theology: birth and formation of the gods, of humans, other species and worlds; it explains the creation of the universe, the place of the human being in that world, the proper relations of Deity with humans, and the ethical mission of individuals and groups, events and organizations of society.

At least three different creations, some traditions say four, others claim five, precede the present world. Each was ruled by its own Sun, and each in turn was destroyed by a different cataclysm according to the myths; these repeat in the religious histories of virtually all Mesoamerican people.

The latest world came into being when the twin gods descended from the heavens with the Earth goddess. Legends say, the two creator gods transformed themselves into giant serpents, grasped the goddess in their coils and tore her in two. With one half they made the new Earth; they took the other half back to the heavens where it brought forth many gods. This correlates to *Inferior Sophia, (Psyche*) and *Superior Sophia, the Mother God*, names that are known in Kabalah.

When these gods saw the *Earth* goddess's mutilated body and heard her cries, they descended to *Earth* to console her. To repay her for her sacrifice, they decreed that from her body would originate all that was needed to sustain the humans that would populate the Earth.

Thus, the new world was made ready for a race of humans, whom *Quetzalcoatl*—venerated as both a god and culture hero—would refashion from the remains of the previous creation into a new awareness. But in the night the wounded goddess continued to cry.

The story as told goes . . . In return for providing sustenance to humanity, she demanded that she be sustained not only by the dead buried in the Earth, but also with the hearts and blood of living victims. Throughout human history the concept of human sacrifices or shedding of blood has been deemed necessary for the continuation of life. It is believed the idea became rooted in our psyches through generations as hunters. It existed in Maya annuals until the introduction of new concepts later in this fourth world, as we will see. While the higher philosophy was introduced in the classic Maya teachings, the shock of bloody sacrifice continued even into the time of the Spaniards.

Hunbatz shared that a blood sacrifice was required of the rulers. There is an 8th century Maya, a richly dressed noblewoman who pierces her tongue with a spiked cord, while the ruler holds a torch over her head.

Stingray spines were also commonly used in *blood-letting rituals* for the purpose of nourishing the gods and to make contact with the supernatural. Some scholars now propose that extreme pain most likely caused *hallucinations,* which may explain why the Maya are so adamant that they could actually speak to their gods.

Also we learned the male leaders of communities or temples used Stingray spines to pierce their penises and shed blood for their people's well-being. They would bleed on paper, show their people the stain, and then burn the paper in a holy ritual, as was the blood of the noblewomen. Thus, the royal couple had sacrificed their own blood for their people; other self-mutilating acts are rumored.

In this 8th century Maya, a richly dressed noblewoman pierces her tongue with a spiked cord, while the ruler holds a torch over her head.

An interesting respect is shown in cemeteries of the Maya. Special areas are set aside for warriors who have given their lives for their people and marking these designated areas are nicely designed stones (usually some war weapons). There are also areas set aside with special cares and engravings (usually of skulls indicating transformation) for women who died in childbirth or as a result of child bearing . . . for they too are honored for having given their lives for their people.

Hunbatz Men admitting, some human sacrifices did occur, much symbology is speaking of the death of the carnal self as the feathered serpent emerges. He makes a point of trying to change the image of the Mayas from *bloodthirsty* to that of respect for life, noting that some human sacrifices were performed also from a position of great honor. He blames most of the bloodthirsty stories largely on the Aztecs culture. The Maya saw blood as sacred and blood-letting as sacred acts, for the good of the people.

A major difference also arises between Mesoamerican religious ideas. The Aztec claim the Fifth World is ending: the Mayas claim we are ending the Fourth, and the Fifth is to come. Both agree the next era is to be one *"of Illumination."* The Mayas themselves believe we are entering a *new world* and Quetzalcoatl will return to lead us into *illumination*. There are many similarities and differences between the Indian people of North and South America, but all acknowledge the ending of a *world*.

There is a parable told occasionally by Aluna Joy Yaxk'in about the Eagle and it's rebirth, I share it now. Not so many know an Eagle goes through transformation as well as people do. It seems there are many reasons it is a sacred bird for America; this is another good reminder. The Eagle can live to 70 or 80 years old; when mid-life occurs, it has a crisis. It has been maturing for years but now its beak and nails have grown until they are crippling. Its wing feathers are so overgrown; it can hardly fly. Now the eagle has to either *change or die*. It cannot fly well so it takes a last flight to the mountains to find a cave in which it can turn its attention inward.

In this protected place it dies or begins again. It must grind its beak down on a rock; it must pull out its overgrown feathers and talons. It must bear the pain of tearing its out-grown body into a more sleek form so that months later it can emerge healed and with new feathers . . . ready to begin again. The eagle has been renewed. The Eagle has now been prepared to enter its new life.

Likewise Humankind is ready for its rebirth; we are to die to the old and be reborn as a new and more divine species. For our world to change; we must change. Each of us has to rework our own beliefs and ideas to form a renewed human collective. These last few years have been our time in the rebirth process. We have heard repeatedly how important it is to turn our attention inward and learn to hear the voice of inner renewal.

If we remember the caterpillar that will turn into a butterfly or the dragonfly that must leave the safety of the water to become what it is meant to be, we, too, must surrender into our unique role in the new world. Transformation must be experienced or we will die.

With the coming of a new world, we must *surrender* to the higher self and listen inward. We must grow into our potential and we can put it off no longer.

With our "flawed" nature our biggest test is "*group trust*". We must go to the cliff and fly. We have to see if we have what it takes to move ahead. For centuries we have been learning life's lessons step by step and now we get the test. A test, yes, but we have met all the trials and lessons, one at a time. *Humanity—We—are gradually transforming* and the only one that does not know it is ourselves.

The Fifth World is here. We know not what it means. But the ancient wise ones told us what they could. They dealt with their limited understanding as best they could and looking ahead they saw the feathered serpent waiting for us. They knew transformation was coming. The past worlds have provided experience for us; we are now ready for the *New Era or the Itza World.* Like an infant in the womb, birth will be embraced. We are moving away from time, space and dimension as we have known them. The soon-to-be-here world is a new world and it will take the wisdom gleaned from the previous worlds to equip us for a new beginning. We begin again.

We will realize we live in a world that is truly alive—everything is a *"reflection"* of the dynamic spark of Life made manifest. We will see Life in a new way in every kingdom; with our senses expanded we will know how to acknowledge Life with its intelligence and expression. *We see Science taking us in this direction* today and many native traditions have protected their wisdom traditions, until now. They have honored the four-leggeds with-out judgment and in time we shall as well.

Illumined persons will no longer play games of "use and abuse" with each other or other kingdoms. They will respect all life in its many shapes and colors. Life-in-harmony will love Father Sun and Mother Earth, its Elders and Wise Ones. World upon worlds will be welcomed; be it Cosmic or Earthly, animal or tree . . . gradually love will become the true nature.

We will come to think of younger kingdoms as the *younger members of the family*. They will be loved as now some love their pets, their flowers, their gems or crystals. A new consciousness is dawning and it is no wonder so often the new world is called the "new day". We can only partially imagine this as of yet. The Fifth World exists in the beauty of the imagination; but it draws near. We must image the higher world working its magic and like a fairy godmother showing us new possibilities.

Ponder for a minute: Perhaps such as been experienced from time to time in places where the ancient ones anchored the memory. Can this be why the story of Atlantis lingers within humanity's group mind or the stories of fairy lands? Iceland with its little people remembers and Ireland as well. I think of Wales and the idea of *"Walking between the worlds"*. This is old language for the mists and valleys that transform people.

Likewise could Shamballa, the White Mountain or the Gobi, even the Hollow Earth, be holy places that retain miraculous tales to gently remind us that there is a better way to live? We will remember to remember and to embrace new possibilities with grateful hope. Were these stories buried deep within to be stir humanity from time to time so it could be inspired to believe the *Consciousness Shift* truly is our next reality?

Familiar Aztec Calendar

The Aztec and the Maya use the same stone calendar. A 52—year cycle was utilized by most of the ancient people. The most fearful time was the end of a designated 52-year period; it was at such a time the Spaniards arrived. Expecting the return of Quetzalcoatl, as prophesied by the old legends, Cortes was mistaken for the legendary Quetzalcoatl when he took his men ashore at Veracruz, Mexico. By the time the Indians realized their mistake, it was too late.

The old religion was then cloaked in Christianity and adapted as possible. Everywhere when old goddesses emerged, they morphed into Mother Mary and the Sun-god became Christ Jesus. The cross became the *holy tree*. The rural Indians had no difficulty embracing the Christian faith with its similar symbols, a history of sacrificial services and the crucifixion. It all seemed very familiar.

Only eleven years after Cortes arrived in 1531, on the site of a destroyed Mayan temple dedicated to a young goddess, a lovely lady appeared in a vision to a poor, simple Indian convert. She asked in native tongue that a temple be built here on the hillside in her honor. Her cult swept throughout the Mexican countryside and eventually to all of Spanish America. We know her now as Our Lady of Guadalupe, Patron Saint of the Americas.

An apparition of a Maya Priestess or Goddess stood on the stones of a torn-down Mayan Temple at Tepeyac where she was once honored. Christians had destroyed her shrine as they came into power, and many of the stones had been carried away to be placed in the new building dedicated to the God of the invaders. Her heart was heavy, she grieved, and as Jose Diego, an old Mayan Indian passed by, she called out to him.

She wanted him to do something for her. Asking what, he was told to carry a message to the bishop within the city telling him she wanted a new shrine built for her. He said, "No, he could not," knowing the dangers of such actions. Her persuasion persisted for several days, and one day he finally agreed to go see the bishop. Of course, the bishop laughed telling the old Indian, now he was a Christian and to give up such ideas. The bishop told Jose, should he see her again to tell her she should send the bishop a sign.

Then on the morning of December 12, 1531, Jose Diego passed the destroyed temple once again. Roses were blooming out of season in the chilly, cactus-covered hillside, and there was the goddess calling to him. She told Jose to take the roses to the bishop; she was not going to hear "no." Gathering them into his tilma, a coarse garment woven from cactus fiber and worn knotted over one shoulder, he gathered them, and the priestess who, he said, rearranged them, tied the ends of his cloak around his neck.

"This is the sign that you are to take to the lord bishop", she said. "Do not let anyone see what you are carrying; do not unfold your mantle until you are in the bishop's presence." Jose trembling obeyed and goes to the bishop's residence.

The rest is history. He unfolds his mantle in the presence of the bishop and other witnesses, the out-of-season roses fell to the floor and as those present gasped, Jose looks to see what they see, and inside his robe is the image of a woman—head bowed, hands folded in prayer, dressed in pink and blue-green, standing on a crescent supported by an angel with a radiant golden sunburst behind her—all imprinted on his tilma.

The Mayans claim the apparition to be the Corn Goddess and the golden sunburst behind her to be a ripen ear of corn . . . It certainly looks more like an ear of corn than an aura for which it has been mistaken. The word Guadalupe *is actually the Spanish rendering of an Aztec word spoken by the Lady herself; it is what she wished to be called. A conquered people in a region where the Catholic religion was perceived by the native populace as foreign, white, and European, the Virgin appeared dark-skinned and spoke native language; the results were electrifying.*

The same garment with image intact is still there in the modern Basilica of Our Lady of Guadalupe, which is built on the site of the destroyed Tepeyac Temple and is a vital shine visited by many tourists, Spanish, Mexican and Mayans—some who know its background and others that do not.

Introducing the Feathered Serpent

It is probable that the first Quetzalcoatl was a god or king of the Atlanteans whose worship was brought to the Western Hemisphere by fugitives from Atlantis. Quetzalcoatl, whose name means "feathered or plumed or precious serpent," and Tezcatlipoca (Tes-cat-li-Poka/Smoking Mirror) came as two mighty forces to vie for power in the world of humanity. As in the case of Zoroaster, several different accounts exist of the life and final departure of Quetzalcoatl. They were probably several different people forming a composite being. Through all the contradictions, we may dimly perceive Quetzalcoatl as a great and noble man, founder of a widespread faith, high priest of sacred mysteries, scientist, mystic and philosopher.

Most frequently we see the sculpture of the serpents head adorned with feathers and or planetary symbols to represent the teachings and responsibilities of becoming an enlightened person. In some places we see a carving as at Chichen Inza depicting the head of the initiate in the mouth of the feathered serpent recognizing the sleeping power within each, to bring the lower self to the point of new desired awareness . . . that of Holy consciousness. Below we see the statue of the Initiate in foreground and the pyramid of Kukulcan in the distance.

Initiate with pyramid in the distance

The Pyramid of Kukulcan is the largest and most important ceremonial structure of Chichen Inza. This 90 foot pyramid is believed to be from the 11th-13th century, built directly upon the foundation of previous temples. This is the location where the inner play of the Sun and the edges of the stepped terraces create the famous shadow display of the Serpent moving on the steps.

European culture emphasis how to live a materialistic existence, but little spiritual truth is preserved and often hard to find. However, in the sacred centers of the Earth it is preserved, waiting for the Maya to conduct sacred ceremonies.

Wisdom teachings tell us we must come to know the seven forces that govern the body and to understand their purpose in keeping with natural and cosmic law. The Maya student of consciousness must learn the use of and understanding of the movement of the Sun with its governing laws.

The time is now for the building of the Light Body. Most call it the Etheric double: The Egyptian's called it the *Ka*. To the Maya it is the Light body because its radiance expresses in and through the wiser ones. This is not the Astral body, but another more subtle vehicle . . . One that becomes an outlet for the solar mind, AHAU, which is purely electromagnetic or fifth-dimensional and knows no time. The solar lords constitute this etheric body of the planet, and they resonate to both the planets' electromagnetic field and its inner-dimensional crystal core of the Earth. They interface, we would say, between human mind and planetary divine mind.

Thus the evolving DNA is most often said to be utilized by the Maya as an acceleration of the naturally evolving DNA (allowing the integration of the group mind). It is said to be measured by the collapse in time it takes one human to communicate to another about halfway around the globe, and is said to be accompanied by concurrent increase in population. Once maximum acceleration is achieved—when communication is electronic and virtually instantaneous—it becomes synchronization: the equally exponential rate of linking up every single human with each other through the utilization of a planetary exo-nervous system. Now, a unified planetary consciousness is attained.

The purpose of this speeded-up frequency is to accelerate the evolving DNA into this planetary exo-nervous system. This will activate a psi-bank, a new mental envelope and memory program for the planet. Our fourth dimension vehicle will be developed and consciousness will expand. When this is achieved, we will recover from separatism and truly know we are One. We will *know* Gaia to be *a living organism with a mental sheath created of human minds.*

Once this synchronization (link-up) is accomplished, the exo-nervous system falls away, to be replaced by the more efficient medium of telepathy. At that point, the Maya materials claim, the planet will be initiated into the Galactic Federation. Our planet will be a sacred planet; it will have passed the tests necessary to receive initiation, and its mind (humanity) will be one mind. Hunbatz Men says this is a "good theory," maybe it will prove so.

As I learned in Peru we are moving into a shift from the masculine energy directing the life of the planet to a time of incoming feminine energy that will restore a balance to the current conditions.

Wisdom teachings have called Shamballa the home of the Divine Masculine, Will and we have sought to be in harmony with Higher Will. This energy has been based in the Himalayas and now the incoming Feminine is awaking in the Andes. This movement that has begun is a stirring of the Planetary Kundalini. Its purpose is to check the misuse of Masculine Force—to balance between the masculine and feminine energies—necessary to restore health to the Planet.

The Planetary Kundalini is stirring from the southern tip of South America and traveling upward through what is called the "*Ring of Fire*", as it is known. It is responsible for earthquakes and the breaking up of crystallizations throughout the dimensions. It is to clear the "illusion" by which we live our lives. It is considered hard on thought forms, false concepts or distorted ones, our bodies and unsupportive life-styles. It is to do away with separative ideas and to lead to our recognition of "*Right Relationships*".

Humanity has certainly transcended some of the limitations with which it has falsely identified. We now identify more with the importance of the kingdoms of nature. Each five-year period has carried us forward toward the mind of an awakened One. We certainly are more aware of higher-mind-possibilities through technology, scientific research and education than we were in 1987. We still lack progress in sensitive areas of perception, intuition and trusting our inner resources.

Quetzalcoatl's mystery cult was served by a hierarchy of priests, who termed themselves "serpents," who consecrated themselves as the *sons of the Snake*. A reference to a subterranean passageway, said to be leading to the roots of heaven, is called the "*snake's hole.*" In other words, the mysteries were only for the initiates—those in whom the kundalini is awakened. Each tradition has a reason the *snake or serpent* is used for a name of the initiate. Remember, *be ye as wise as a serpent and as gentle as a dove.*

The stories of Quetzalcoatl have all the elements of a cosmic myth skillfully treated, with definite emphasis upon the theological and astrological aspects. There are stories concerning a place of reeds which can only be reached by water, and a drawing of Aztlan, an island surrounded by dashing waves with a high mountain rising in the middle. Some connect this with Atlantis, some with *Asia* others are reminded of the *story of Moses.*

The Miraculous Conception of Quetzalcoatl

On a certain day, three sisters were sitting together in their home, when in their midst a heavenly apparition appeared, so fearsome two sisters died of fright. The spirit addressed the third sister, who remained calm. The spirit said it "came as an ambassador from the god of the Milky Way, to search on Earth for a virgin, to bear a son, to be called Quetzalcoatl." The father was the great god, OMetecutli (OM-ay-tay-coot-lee) called the "lord of our flesh," and who was the direct creator of humanity. (Notice, the first two letters of the name are, O M.)

The god overshadowed the virgin with his breath, impregnating her; Quetzalcoatl was born of a Divine father and a human mother. When the child was born, his birth was accompanied with many mysterious omens and wonders in the heavens, as always with a Divine incarnation. The record is silent on his childhood years. According to most stories, he appeared at Veracruz, either riding upon a raft of serpents, or being carried in a canoe made of snakes.

He is generally represented as a man of mature years, a patriarch with a long beard and fair, white skin. When pictured upon the raft, he is covered from shoulders to feet in a robe covered with white crosses. Upon his head is a magnificent bonnet of quetzal plumes; he carried a magic wand and performs wonders, as ascribed to Moses' sacred staff.

The story tells us, the people were suffering a drought and famine when he came to power. Knowing ignorance was the cause of distress in the world, he taught the people ways to create an orderly life. He instituted sacrifices to the gods and revived interest in spiritual matters. His offerings were of no avail, however, until he offered this suffering to the deities. The self-inflicted wounds appeased the heavenly wrath only after he hung himself from a branch of the Tree of Life and wounded himself with its thorns.

When the gods accepted his sacrifice, the Valley of Mexico bloomed as a rose, and all good things came to the people. During his reign, Quetzalcoatl continued to instruct his people. His influence was kind; the people were happy. At his command, the Earth teemed with fruits and flowers without the pain of work. Legend has it that an ear of Indian corn grew to be as much as one could carry; this compared to the concept of the land of milk and honey (Exodus 3:8), or the bounty of oversized fruit. Cotton is said to have taken on the colors of rich dyes of human art as it grew. Quetzalcoatl ruled in the capacity of a priest, rather than a king.

The stories of his personal life contain great contradictions. Some declare he was a celibate initiate; other stories refer to a consort. It is said he placed princes on the throne and remained aloof from temporal entanglements. Some stories tell of fasting, and then, there is the cup given to him from which to drink in a mystical sacrament. Natives had a ceremony in which they made a model of his body from dough. While it baked, they divided it among themselves and ate with great solemnity. Legends claim he brought upon himself the wrath of the priesthood of the previous era for delivering his people from the bondage of ignorance and superstition.

A story in a Vatican Codex quotes from Lord Kingsborough:

"*Here are numerous representations of the crucified god with curious marks resembling nail wounds in his hands and feet.*" The seventy-third page of the codex is the most remarkable of all, for Quetzalcoatl is not only represented as crucified upon a cross of Greek form, but his burial and descent into hell are also depicted in a very curious manner. "*After forcing the lord of the underworld to pay him homage, Quetzalcoatl rises from the grave.*"

The Story Resumes:

In the legends, Tezcatlipoca, or "Smoking Mirror," (in English), elects to be the adversary of Quetzalcoatl and determines to break the power of the magician-priest. Translated as "Smoking Mirror," we might think of this as one's "shadow." Assuming the appearance of an elderly man, he gains an audience. As an elder, he prescribes a remedy for the aged holy one. The medicine was an intoxicating drink which numbed Quetzalcoatl's senses. The story evidently intends to convey that the evil spirit of negativity drugged the empire and brought about its destruction from within. Here we are reminded that wherever bright light shines, darkness is attracted and attempts to put out the light.

The legend records Quetzalcoatl as remaining with his people until the empire was so demoralized that it was no longer possible to maintain the integrity of the people. He left only to return to the mysterious place from which he came. Departing, he set out in his advanced years to destroy the buildings and to hide his treasures. He changed rich trees to bushes and ordered all of the birds of plumage and song to quit the valley and follow him. Thus, he left the land as he found it—a desert.

In one account, he traveled for twenty years; in another, he went to the water and called to the sea, and his skiff of serpents appeared above the water. He made a prophecy that was to prove the future undoing of the empire. He said, he would return in a later time; his descendants were to establish the next great age which would bring with it the permanent paradise of which the Eden he had invoked by magic was but a taste. Stepping onto his raft, he disappeared over the mysterious horizon, returning to his father. When the Spaniards arrived, this legend caused the natives to welcome them and to hope the return of Quetzalcoatl was at hand.

We should review two other accounts of his death—each quite different. In the first, the aged prince died full of years and honored for his wisdom. His body was carried in a stately procession to the peak of the highest mountain where it was consumed by divine flames descending from heaven, as in the passing of Zoroaster. As the flames surrounded his body, there appeared in the midst of the flames a bird of such magnificence that its plumage darkened the flames by contrast. It was the spirit of Quetzalcoatl ascending to heaven in the royal guise of the peacock.

A still different account is given by Lewis Spence who writes: Quetzalcoatl cast himself upon a funeral pyre and was consumed. And that ashes rising upward changed into a multitude of birds of brilliant plumage to fill the jungles. His heart soared into heaven and became the morning star, *Venus*. And so upon him was bestowed the title, the "*Lord of the Dawn*". Even today, Maya ruins abound with temples dedicated to Venus. Of course, both stories bear a resemblance to the Resurrecting-Phoenix and perennial wisdom.

These legends were well known by *Montezuma*, who was surrounded by seers and prophets. Signs which appeared in the heavens, we are told, warned the emperor that the conquistadors with their horses and guns were not emissaries from the Sun-god, but were plundering mortals with an eye for loot.

Hunbatz Men Blessing a group with Carol Parrish and Alan Okin. *This is an impressive temple receiving-area for initiates, and the site of an extraordinary photo taken in an initiation rite done by Hunbatz Men in January 1993.*

Guatemala

Even today, particularly in Guatemala, one can see the two faiths merged into one. At a Christian (Catholic) church Chichicastenango midwife's, medicine men and women, herbalists and shamans bring their goods herbs, medicine, and alcohol for medicinal purposes to be blessed in the aisles of the church during services. In this way, it is easy to see how significant the blending is of the Mayan and Christian faiths throughout the ages.

In the shot below, we see the steps of an ancient pyramid which has been taken apart and these last steps used to make the foundation of a Christian Church. The picture shows us the many steps the Maya still claim as the place of worship. They cover the steps with candles and flowers daily, while the church pictured behind them is entered from the side by the Christians and serves their congregation from that angle. Here you see a few travelers venturing onto the steps with Maya people after our visit to the church.

Carol E. Parrish-Harra Ph. D.

Steps to Santo Tomas Church, Chichicastenango, Guatemala

Section II: How the Quest Began

My personal "Maya quest" began Sunday, July 14, 1985 in New York State. I awakened early in the morning, excitedly happy and stimulated after a dream. My excitement and exhilaration are hard to put on paper. I knew instantaneously this dream was vitally important and could talk of nothing else for several hours. The dream had to be significant. This unusual dream resulted in the discovery of the approaching date of what we now know as Harmonic Convergence.

In 1985 while participating in a retreat in New York State, I was awakened by a profound dream. I rushed to a friend's door to awaken him. I needed his insights. Ben Osborne and I shared experiences we didn't discuss with just anyone. Intuitive and knowledgeable, he surely could help me uncover the message. My heart raced as I awakened exhilarated, a sense of urgency surging through me. The dream etched vividly into my head.

A spiritual teacher from Atlanta, Georgia, Ben Osborne, often spent holidays with my husband and me. It was early when I knocked at his door, but I couldn't rest. It seemed prophetic that he was here now. We discussed the dream for several hours and agreed on its significance.

From my earliest meditation experiences, a "peacock fan" would appear and spread to fullness in my mind's eye, and then other impressions would follow. It had come to signal *truthfulness* to me.

> *I am writing at a simple desk in the chapel in Florida, my place for spiritual work. Distracted by a sound, I turn. The room is without furniture. A small snake lies on the floor. I examine it, get a tool, pick it up, and take it outside. Deciding it is dead, I throw it into the bushes. Another snake appears the same size and very still, with little, if any, life in it. Again, this time I used a long-handle, branch-cutters (loppers) to remove the snake.*
>
> *Returning to my desk to write, I hear another odd sound. Now, standing at the back of the room is a large "secretary"—the kind of desk whose door lowers for a writing surface.*
>
> *As I watch this door bump and bulge from within, a huge snake, larger around than a person's arm, emerges. I rush to hold the desk door shut, trying to prevent the snake's escape.*

I push against the door, but the head and about 10 inches of the body emerge. It is so powerful I can barely hold it in. Examining it, I hear myself say, "This is a feathered serpent. Oh, I've heard of the feathered serpent. This is important. I should know what this means." I keep saying, "I know this is very important. I know I should know its significance."

As I repeat these words and observe the details of this magnificent creature—covered with blues and greens, the perfection of its feathers lying neatly against its body—three smaller feathered serpents emerge from either side of the desk. They are partially out and flailing in the air—seven snakes striving to get free. The peacock has been a profound personal symbol for me for over two decades. Seeing the "eyes" of myriad peacock feathers on the snakes, I know this is an important message.

I am not afraid, just profoundly interested. The incredible beauty kindles awe, and I feel electrically charged.

The rich feelings of the dream stayed with me for hours. I knew vaguely some of the story of Quetzalcoatl and came home from New York to research the subject. Thus began my quest for Quetzalcoatl. The dream came in time to awaken me to Harmonic Convergence and to the world-wide significance of this time period. And to allow me to both share my insights with others, and mostly to prepare myself and those with whom I could awaken the ways, to participate actively with the Higher World, preparing itself for the age change and the return of Quetzalcoatl.

Knowing all ancient wisdom stories have a returning hero, I recall how all people love their Creator in their own way. I seek the grace to remember. Knowing vaguely some of the story of Quetzalcoatl, the Mayan feathered serpent, I began to quest to know more. Six months later I was in Peru asking for information. By January 1986, a group of us, 22 in fact, went to Peru and asked for the legend of Quetzalcoatl.

It was there I heard of the approaching significant date of August 16 and 17, 1987. I heard about the forthcoming August, l987 date and that it was supposedly a trigger date. I was told of a Mayan teacher by the Peruvian shamans who spoke good English, lived in Mexico, and often traveled to the U.S. I knew to go to Mexico to find the many Maya Legends that are, in fact, parables, to begin to find the Maya wisdom. I believe my dream was counseling me to throw out smaller, lifeless "knowledge," to study and write (the secretary) about this Mayan legend (the snakes).

In Peru we had many examples of phenomena, but most important was a guideline the shamans offered: *When the Condor and the Eagle flies together, peace will abide.* Important as well, was the explanation that the base of the planetary kundalini grounded in the Himalayas was shifting to the Andes. Since that time the work of Jose Trigueirinho has explained much, claiming the feminine flow has begun.

Bringing the highest energy on the planet to South America, now based in the Andes (moving from the Himalayas where it had been for centuries), these two now act as polar opposites in the same way as the North and South poles. Thus we see the new era is being born in the West. It is to be called the Age of the Flowers; the meaning is that people are to "bloom," the flowers being the chakras.

I came home determined to find Hunbatz Men, the Mayan Prince, who was sharing Mayan wisdom, but as always had to bide my time. I first found him at a workshop in Washington State, and from there I received a Mexican address and learned Hunbatz's home base was in Merida, Mexico, but he was rarely there. I wrote several times, and while waiting discovered the work of Tony Shearer, a Lakota artist of many talents, storyteller, author, poet, and playwright a native poet, and read *"Beneath the Moon and Under the Sun."* Tony Shearer was the first I found referring to the up-coming dates of the Maya Calendar. Later, as I followed his work, I really learned how prolific he was and how he had slipped the forthcoming events into his poetry. He provided more insights to the new time in *"The Lord of the Dawn."* Tony awakened Jose' Arguelles to these ideas, and even though he has received little public recognition for his role, Tony, a Native American, facilitated the awakening of many in his book, *Lord of the Dawn: Quetzalcoatl.*

During a visit with Tony, telling him about the village, our appreciation of the Maya teachings, and how we admired his work, he said he was the first to publish a known time schedule unlocking the secrets of the Mesoamerican tradition. He said it was kept hidden for the protection of the native people, and only now is spirit telling them they are to share for the time has come. He warns us to go carefully with native people for they have little reason to trust their conquerors, or to share or even to assist us, but we can learn with due respect from their wisdom.

Tony wrote a number of books about the mysteries of the Maya tradition. Another artist and creative thinker, Jose Arguelles, attracted the world attention with their contributions, introductions, and explanations of the Maya calendar.

Jose Arguelles, (1939—2011) an art historian who became world-renown as an author, visionary, and educator, as well as creator of Earth Day, initiates Harmonic Convergence and names the 25-year span that we are now ending *"Campaign for the Earth"*. He announced the criticalness of these 25 years between 1987—2012 to the world as a revealed-to-be-discovered shift hidden in the Maya Calendar.

Now, as we rapidly approach an ending, and thus "New Beginning," confusion results because the Maya Calendar is running out (ending) he called the last date *"the end of the Earth,"* and warned us that we must find a new awareness of how to live in the last days and be prepared for mighty change.

Since the Calendar left for us is round and few understand how to read it. Certainly in many aspects he was correct, as are the many others speaking to us about creating new attitudes and changing our foolish and thoughtless ways.

However, the mistake in this understanding is that the Maya Calendar, being correct is round, and when it finishes it reaches what has been called the end of the calendar, it merely rolls on around the curve to begin a new cycle, just like a repeat of old configurations but on a higher spiral. We will continue to be challenged to find solutions, to work on relationships, and to build a civilization based on wiser assumptions than we could generate on the previous spiral. References to "*The Age of Flowers*" acknowledge the blooming of the chakras as continuing the development of the human being in his/her potential. Each ring around the calendar could be thought of as a world. We must realize in the Maya tradition it does not mean "*end of the earth*" but "*end of a world view.*"

The steps began; researching, planning, and preparation. Soon I made progress in my search for Hunbatz Men and was able to discuss with him the mystery of the feathered serpent and to learn more about the "soon-to—be-acknowledged" message of the Mayan People regarding the forthcoming Harmonic Convergence. Eagerly, I began preparations for myself and others who could be awakened to the magnitude of this message. I sought to understand it, and longed to learn how to participate in this worldwide happening.

There is a similarity in the Maya material that is much like the Buddhists that says, "*Remember to Remember.*" It teaches at all times, remember who you are and why you are here. The Popol Vuh say, the *only reason people were put here was to sing and give praise to the gods. That they are to rejoice in the garden the gods arranged for them. Their work is to sing like the birds . . . to praise and give glory.*

Picture of Hunbatz Men, *SHV newsletter*

I was excited to celebrate Harmonic Convergence at my home, Sparrow Hawk Village, Tahlequah, OK, and arranged eleven days of celebration at that significant time, as proposed by so many of these experts. In pulling these comments together, I used the proposed ideas of Hunbatz Men, Jose Arguelles, and Tony Shearer. There was little information at that time, so we published suggestions, ways and means for acknowledging the forthcoming world-wide event.

After August I7 and 18, 1987, other significant events will continue to occur that kept me keyed into the importance of the Maya mysteries. I continued to prepare myself and others by exposing as many as possible, with trips to Maya Land, and with frequent visits of Hunbatz Men to Sparrow Hawk Village. Large turn-outs gathered to hear him, understanding ever more clearly the message of the transition time between Harmonic Convergence and the magical date December 21-22, 2012.

We learned that when Europeans first landed on the shores of Mexico's Yucatan Peninsula early in the 16th century, the great Maya centers were already faded relics, time-honored, worn, overgrown and abandoned. Awe-inspiring remains of more than 60 Maya *"cities"* are simply the most visible and enduring evidence of a civilization spectacular in its achievements. The true dimensions of this unique civilization, however, were lost upon most Spaniards who, in their haste to conquer and convert, failed to comprehend what lay before them.

Not until the 19th century did the grandeur of Maya culture begin to be explored, awakening the world to this high civilization—similar to Ancient Egypt—that flourished years ago on the American continent. In the late 19th century, traditional researchers became very interested in these indigenous people.

I soon discovered the work of two of the most respected ethnologists/translators and historical researchers. Both Ralph L. Roy, *Books of Chilam Balam of Chumayel,* and J. Eric Thompson, *Maya History and Religion,* had dedicated their careers to Maya studies. Knowing the histories were rapidly disappearing, the University of Oklahoma supported these two historians when there was little interest in Mesoamerican culture.

A little fact is that only four Mayan books have survived the Spanish Inquisition. The majority of Mayan history has survived orally, and that is what gives us the remnants we are piecing together. The majority of Maya communities have remained isolated until at least the last three decades. Even today, Guatemala remains more isolated. The Shift of the Ages newsletter 8/26/2011

Later I would connect with the work of Jose Arguelles, and the magnificent *Mayan Factor* was published. All of these earlier inspired persons were artists, and in some way through their art work told the world what was coming. Recall how challenging it was at that time to comprehend the emerging ideas; many scoffed at Harmonic Convergence and the ideas with which we are now well accustomed.

And another lucky find was an interesting and somewhat different kind of reference about Quetzalcoatl in a rare book *Agharta: The Subterranean World,* by Raymond Bernard. See excerpt below (page 29):

> *That these Aghartan Teachers or Buddha's came from the Subterranean World by flying saucer is indicated in the case of one such teacher—Quetzalcoatl, a tall, fair, bearded prophet who appeared among the Aztec and Mayan Indians of Mexico, Yucatan and Guatemala many centuries before the coming of the first white man. The Aztecs called him "God of Abundance" and the "Morning Star." His name Quetzalcoatl, means "Feathered Serpent," meaning a teacher of wisdom (symbolized by the serpent) who flew (symbolized by the serpent being feathered). This meant that he came to these Indians on a flying saucer from the Subterranean World of Agharta through the North polar opening. Tradition says that he vanished (on a flying saucer) and spent eight days in the Subterranean World (in the hollow interior of the Earth). He taught the Mayas identical doctrines of Aghartan philosophy as those taught by the Buddha's in Asia, including non-killing (vegetarianism and pacifism), continence, etc.*

As I continued to study I noted many of the materials had something on the Hollow Earth theory. This idea is not restricted to Maya but exists in "Folk Lore" in many cultures. It offers ideas that the Subterranean Worlds will teach some Rainbow Warriors to travel through underground tunnels. According to Hopi Legend, some of them survived past destruction by living in the Earth, and when this World began, they were told to come to the service of the Earth and become its guardian. The union of the subterranean race and the races living upon the Earth's surface will recognize and reflect inner and outer harmonies in each life form.

Elizabeth Van Buren in her book, "Land of White Waters" has much to say about sacred links between the Himalayas and the Andes and includes throughout her book droplets concerning the capital of Argatha (The Hollow Earth Theory), even going so far as to say, that Nicholas Roerich stated, a Lama told him Argatha and Lhassa are joined spiritually and physically. "Naga" is the word for the culture of the snake taught by the Maya to the people of Tibet and it is still taught. Naga Maya means everything is beautiful; somewhat like how to live the beautiful life, so says Hunbatz.

From Chapter Four: *Argatha, The Subterranean World (Page 30)*

> *Quetzalcoatl is described as being "a man of good appearance and grave countenance, with a white skin and beard, and dressed in a long flowing white garment." He was called by some Quetzalcoatl and by other, Huemac, because of his great goodness. He taught the Indians the way of virtue by his word and deed. He hoped to save them from vice and to give them laws and counsel and to restrain them from lust and to practice chastity. He instituted a vegetarian diet, with corn as a principal food, fasting and body hygiene. After remaining some time with the Indians, and seeing how little they cared to follow his higher doctrines—though they did follow his recommendation to plant and eat corn—he vanished, telling them that some-day he would return again. Thus, did this "visitor from heaven" (the Subterranean World) leave the same way, returning to the Subterranean World from where he came through the north polar—opening.*

Another interesting piece from the same material about South America follows:

Chapter Six: The Mysterious Tunnels and Subterranean Cities of South America (Page 36)

> *It is claimed that the earth is honeycombed with a network of tunnels, which are especially abundant in South America, and that these tunnels lead to subterranean cities in immense cavities in the earth. Most famous of these tunnels is the Roadway of the Incas: which is said to stretch for several hundreds of miles south of Lima, Peru, via Cuzco . . . Tiahuanaco and the Three Peaks, going on to the Atacambo Desert, where all traces of it is lost. Another branch (of tunnels) that runs to Brazil, where it is connected by tunnels to the coast, here the tunnels go under the bottom of*

the ocean in the direction of the lost Atlantis. In this way Atlantis once had direct connection with its Peruvian colony in the Andes, through tunnels that run under the Atlantic Ocean and then under Brazil, Passing through Panama and Santa Catarina to Matto Grosso and then on to Peru. They then ran down the Andes to Chile. Madame Blavatsky wrote about this Andean tunnel which opened at Africa, in northern Chile.

Later, I would once again connect with the Hollow Earth Theory or penetration to the Inner World, through the work of Jose Trigueirinho. He has much to offer in regard to UFO's and spacial beings penetrating the physical dimension both through the waters of the Seas and the land of the Earth. He has established contact with Light Beings who have exposed to futuristic wisdom ideas. (See his book, *Calling Humanity*, chapters: Cosmic, Intraterrestial and Surface Races and Space Vessels pages 95-101)

Public interest is developing in UFO's, Aliens, and Life in other dimensions within our own society and certainly much more is said privately about such happenings. The USA is one of the most conservative countries in this regard. Whenever we travel to other places, South America being one of the most open, we find interesting stories to hear and think about.

In 1989, I was invited by Alan Feinstein of Operation Indigo to participate in an experiment regarding space contact. It was about a private briefing to be held the previous December at the request of NASA regarding a strange formation discovered on Mars—one resembling a human face. I decided to participate.

All participants were instructed to send two precise thoughts toward an unobstructed view of the sky at a specified synchronized time on June 29, 1989. We were to clear our minds, then at the designated time, look upward, concentrating and repeating the two thoughts for at least a full minute.

When the evening arrived, again, I happened to be at a spiritual retreat; this time in Minnesota. I sat outdoors, as requested. Looking at the sky at 9 PM, it was not quite dark. I did as instructed for five minutes, repeating these thoughts in my mind:
"Is there any way we can communicate?"
"Can you send me a sign of your existence?"

Afterward, I went up to my room, avoiding contact with anyone. We were asked to keep ourselves as clear as possible in our minds and emotions from then to bedtime; right before retiring, repeat the thoughts again and have a pad and pencil ready to record any dream or unusual occurrence. I did not read before sleep so I could keep my mind clear of outside influences.

At 3:00 AM I was awakened, I sat up and got out of my bed. I looked out the window and saw a most peculiar sight. A peacock sitting upright sailed by the window; it was not in a flying mode, but rather like "sitting." The tree outside my window which in fact was below window level seemed behind the shape. When I took out my pad and pen and tried to write down the dream, I had trouble writing because I didn't turn on a light, not wanting to wake up my roommate. It seemed as though I was almost sleep-walking. I went back to bed and fell into a profound sleep.

When I awoke in the morning, I saw the notes and remembered the dream clearly. I recalled getting out of bed, etc., and yet, looking out the window, it looked very different.

I reported all of this in a letter to the Operation Indigo project person and thought, well, they asked for it, and it was unusual.

This seemed to be the end of the story until approximately a year later, Sept. 15, 1990, when a book arrived at the Village Bookstore. It was vibrantly brilliant and I knew immediately it was important to me. I picked it up: *The Flight of the Feathered Serpent* by Peter Balin. When I opened the book, there was almost precisely the picture I had seen in my NASA experience. I was overwhelmed—so much so I photocopied the picture and sent it to Operation Indigo as a follow-up.

The West has overlooked much of its own myths, symbology and legends when it emphasis' institutional and intellectual thinking instead of intuitive, mythological awareness. The group wisdom resides in the myths of the people and in just such a way is delivered to future generations.

An interesting aside: At Well Cathedral, Wells, England, a 12th century beauty, there is a metal sculpture of a Peacock on a cross with the Peacock representing the Christ. From a book of symbology, we learn the peacock was the favorite bird of noble ladies and, as an emblem of beauty and glory; it appeared not only in their gardens, but also on a Roman coin. In some Eastern countries its feather is still a mark of honor. The peacock's tail-feathers full of colorful eyes, forming the beautiful pattern, are the stars and planets of the Hindu universe and a symbol of the "all-seeing" powers of the Christian Church.

As a symbol of Immortality, the peacock was adopted by the Christians through some confusion with the phoenix. Since the bird was unknown in the West, a peacock took its place. It was believed that its flesh never decayed, like the incorruptible Christian soul. A good example of this symbolism is its use by Hieronymus Bosch. In his *Ars Symbolica* he has blended every color into the peacock's tail to express total unity.

Just as symbology about present day happenings, present many unanswerable issues when we seek to understand our modern mythological world, more struggles are created when we attempt to understand the reality of centuries ago.

Interpretations and answering questions around the peculiar hieroglyphs of the ancient Americas form the most acute challenges in present-day archaeology. Researchers struggle to clarify tablets, codices and stone carvings. We often hear, "America is a continent without a history", yet, this is a statement of folly. Stories and mythology flourish with evidence of great civilizations; only our ignorance veils the information.

Lewis Spence wrote *The Myths of Mexico and Peru* in July, 1913 at Edinburgh (published in London by Ballantyne), considered one of the most marvelous books ever written about the unknown people. Born in Scotland and educated in dentistry at Edinburgh University, Spence wrote for the British Weekly before becoming a freelancer. He became fascinated by the civilizations of Mexico and Central America, as well as other sites of mystery religions of the world.

I have a wonderful anecdotal story to tell about his book, *The Myths of Mexico and Peru*. I hunted for this book when I began this research, and it was nowhere to be found; I tried library searches as well as bookstores. One day, after several years, my friend, Grace Bradley, came in and told me she had something for me. Apologizing, she told me she had tried two times to give this book to others, but they wouldn't take it. Yes, you guessed it: this rare and wonderful book by Lewis Spence, noted authority on the Maya was her gift to me. Such a rare treasure I placed it in the Sancta Sophia Library, Sparrow Hawk Village, Tahlequah, OK.

The Creation Story: As interpreted from the *Popol Vuh* and the *Chilam Balam*

Heaven is formed, then Earth and her contents: minerals, vegetables, animal kingdoms, and finally humanity. The progressive order of creation is carried out by a Creator who is the first cause of all that exists.

The *Chilam Balam of Chumayel* declares:

> ". . . *Divinity took out from itself its divinity and made heaven and earth. On two Eb, it made the first ladder descend to the middle of heaven and in the middle of the water.*" (That is the ladder of clouds referred to elsewhere.) Further on: "*All was created by Father God, and by his Word, there, where there was no heaven or earth, was his Divinity, which through its self-made itself into a cloud and created the universe. Its great and divine power and majesty made the heaven's tremble.*
>
> *The one that is Divinity and the Power, brought into being the Great Stone of Grace, there where before was no heaven and from it were born Seven Sacred Stones. Seven warriors suspended it in the spirit of the wind, Seven elected flames, and then seven times were it the seven measures of the night: Further on the seven gods are spoken of in the singular as the "Descendants of Seven Generations, provided by the Eternal, all of which is perfect in accord.*"

After creating and delegating power to the god-seven, the Supreme Being confines itself to the supervision and management of the universe. In order for all to be perfect, the "Head of Heaven" must be integrated into the god-seven to express Divinity through each.

Only now, the Regent-Gods of the four cosmic corners come into being and take their places as the points of the solstices and equinoxes. "Word" and "action" are equivalent terms—used in the same sense by the Maya. Speaking the Word implies instantaneous creation: the deed is done. Remember our story: The meditation of these four builders of the Earth pronounces "light . . . energy," and the earth is formed.

These regents of the Earth are cosmic angels, set at four points of the compass to work in conjunction with earthquakes to bring about the destruction of the world when appropriate. (Their names are Tzakof, (zah-koff), Bital, (bee-tall), Alom, (ah-lom) and Cajolom (kie-ya-lahm.) We know them as Gabri-el, Rapha-el, Uri-el and Micha-el. Remember, in our tradition and Kabalah, "*el*" means "Lord."

The underworld, an inferior cosmic plane, does not come into being until later than the time of creation. However; *The Book of Chilam Balam of Chumayel* records a fight between the beings of the heaven world and those of the underworld. This presents an interesting parallel to the war in which Archangel Micha-el and the heavenly host confront the powers of the lower world, evil.

Quetzalcoatl (also known as Gucamatz and sometimes Kukucan in other South American cultures), is a general name given to the creative forces portrayed as radiating light and covered with a green mantle like the quetzal bird. Gucamatz literally means "serpent-bird," sometimes translated as "serpent with quetzal plumes." The solar ray, as a symbol, indicates divine feathers, or hair with magical properties and are held to be synonymous.

The nature gods clothe themselves in the green mantle (color of vegetation) when involved in a creative act (season of growth). The production of maize is equated with this work. The Elder puts on his ritual suit of "green" to perform marital rituals. When the Hor chan (*or-chon: meaning head of the serpents, leader of the initiates*) puts on his green mantle; he represents the feathered serpent for which he is the Earthly representative. (Very similar to how the priest/minister is compared to the Christ when he is in his official role.)

In the account of *Popol Vuh*, the seven gods convene in heaven to deliberate, offer opinions and views, consult and confer about the future they propose to create, and finally reach a unanimous agreement upon which they can be satisfied. This celestial assembly occurs each time there is to be a major creative opportunity. Could this remind us of the Theosophical Society hierarchy—seven creators—coming together to direct the opportunities of humanity?

The gods spoke as the voice of the Heart of Heaven: "Earth" and she is born. Thus, the Sacred Square or Ground and configuration of the ball game came to be.

The first of the ages is known as the Age of the Giants. In this period, man must struggle against gigantic animals; so stories of a primeval man of huge stature exist here, as well as in the Old Testament. Following the formation of the Earth and its vegetation, the gods proceeded to populate it with animate beings who, in exchange for their having been given life, must worship their Creator. The woods and mountains were covered with animals. Each animal, with its own den, nest or burrow was given means for expression: cries, howls, grunts, separating each group according to its manner of being understood—the basis of differentiating the human kingdom into linguistic groups.

The four cosmic gods, who participate as the owners of wild plants and animals, are the keepers of the woods, just as the human is the guardian of the temple. The woods, as well as, the Temple, are considered Divine. The Indian continues to turn to the Chac (the god) when he needs to hunt an animal, a plant, or a tree; to receive permission he must justify his need and pay for the concession granted by them.

The gods concede life, not as a free gift, but provided only on condition that their creatures acknowledge their dependence upon the Creator and pay tribute. For that reason, the animals are commanded to pronounce the name of Creator since "*we are your mother and father.*" The animals, being unable to comply because they lack fit language, grieve the gods, and lamenting their failure, the gods resolve to exchange these creatures with others. They condemn the animals to have their flesh sacrificed and to be eaten: "*and solely for that reason, all the animals which live on Earth would be killed.*"

Any change from the common word a group employs to designate "Divinity" meets with resistance and creates political separation, for language is unifying within the tribe and their identity. The first human generation tried repeatedly to express its adoration (*to the seven gods*), but because of their differing speech, they failed to understand each other and lost affection for each other, "*and so the Creator did nothing for them.*"

Because humans were ignorant of how to honor the Creator, they were condemned to live in caves and hollows like animals. Deity did nothing for humanity, abandoned to fate. Similarly, Philo spoke of the first creatures of Phoenician cosmology as "*animals without understanding.*"

The *Popol Vuh* states, the first Mesoamericans were ignorant of their origins. They neither worshipped Sun, Moon, stars, nor deity in temples. They lacked sites or ceremonies. They lived without strife or feud and without evil-doing. They set aside places for calling to Deity and kept those very clean. (*Cleanliness remains a requirement for pleasing deity.*) Here they knelt, lifted high their hands and looked to the sky, crying out, "*Where is our father!*" Thus ends World One.

Note: This place for crying out to the higher world remains today as the patio or plaza inseparable from the temple where ultimately multitudes would come to pray for divine favors.

The Second World marks a stage of cultural progress in linguistics, since people "*are able to speak*". Both Maya legends and Quiche sources agree upon the production of poorly formed creatures modeled of damp earth. Peruvian mythology also calls the Creator, "god", that which works or makes with mud. We have in Genesis the reference to man being made from dust.

Another sign of progress is that humanity must struggle in order to procreate and multiply since that is Divine Will. The Second World people multiplied and began to care for and respect fathers, mothers and lords, and to obey them. Progress began in family and family relations. They began to till the soil and had ovens; they had no idols or temples, nor could they weave. They had fruits of the Earth, nuts and seeds." **Thus, the Second World ends.**

Immediately following the destruction of the second creation, the divine four came together to consult. How can we form superior, capable ones *"who can see, understand and invoke us*?" they asked.

Preparation for the Third World begins, and for the first time a *"feminine"* deity appears—Ixmucne (eesh-moo-cah-nay), partner to Ixpiyacoc (eesh-pee-yah-coke), the *"male"* deity. The supreme deity comes forth as a divine pair, called the grandparents of the Maya and the entire human race. Under the personification of the old Lunar-Earth goddess, the matriarchal horticultural stage begins.

After selecting the Regent, the Chacs (lords) come together again to determine what kinds of human begins would be formed and sustained; the requirement this time is that now these beings were to adore them as superiors. Legends or teaching stories attempt to explain that humanity is an eternal debtor and should praise the gods if Divine protection is desired.

The Moon, her function is as the Mistress of the World (the lunar goddess), and the rain chac work in unison, to pour down celestial favors to benefit humanity. Rains are/ were indispensable to the success of planting, so we now see why the Lords of rain and astronomy observations become increasingly important. The worship of a lunar goddess begins a system of time computation.

In the *Chiam Balam* we read:

> When anciently the world was not awakened . . . the Moon was born and began to walk alone . . . . After the Month was born, it created the one called "Day" (the Lunar Mother gave birth to one called "Day"). This one walked with the mother . . . .

Here is authentic testimony to the establishment of the lunar calendar before the solar calendar, and of the matrilineal state. Astrology is established as is divination with grains of corn, and (Ixpiyacoc/ masculine and Ixmucne/feminine) the grandparents of the Maya appear.

The Third World of Creation begins. The feminine deity is active; the masculine is not. Beans and corn become important and are seen as companions reflecting the dual grandparents. Beans are feminine; corn is masculine. The maize god is introduced and will come to power in the Fourth Creation when the patriarchal agrarian comes to age. The bean is the principal food of the Third State.

In this era, notes the *Chilam Balam of Chumayel, "sons had no fathers, mothers no husbands."*

The creatures of the third Era mated and reproduced, but had no heart or feelings (*no bonds*), and were unaware they were sons/daughters of the Creator. They wandered about like strangers without purpose. They were unable to know and understand the *Heart of Heaven*. They could speak, but used their mouth only for eating. People multiplied rapidly and migrated, diffusing families here and there.

The gods resolved to destroy the beings of the third creation, condemning them to disappear by dying, for they gave the gods no praise . . . For the first time *"death"* appears; it happened that Deity, Our Father, invented the first death. A great flood came to wipe out the beings of the Third World. Resin fell from the heavens (an allusion to frequent volcanic cataclysms for the original territory of the Maya). Now a *god of death* is introduced. The *Popol Vuh* has even the animals and household implements helping to destroy the people. **As the Third World ends**, the earthen jars, pans, bowls, pots, dogs and chickens reproach their masters for their mistreatment and misuse. The Indian learns to treat his animals and belongings with respect.

The Fourth World begins to form: Until this time only very little light was found on Earth because Sun did not exist as now. The faces of Sun and Moon were still covered.

Most believe this is a reference to the spiritual darkness on the planet in the prehistoric periods, perhaps living out of the collective unconscious in contrast to the later era of true culture of the Maya (*the Fourth Period*) when the gods uncovered their faces.

The forces of heaven—Hunab P'u (*male*) and Ixbalamque (eesh-bah-lom-kay) (*female*)—*"twins"*—are the grandchildren of the earlier deities. She is the new Moon Goddess for the fourth period, and he, the Sun and Son of the Creator of All. The struggle between the gods and giants represents the forces of Heaven and Earth telling us cosmic harmony did not yet rule. Now new morality is modeled. The macro family provides sages, and all the arts are passed to humanity.

The ball game is introduced and takes its place in history. In fact, the diamond with four corners representing Chacs is followed by a fifth seated in the cave, or underground chamber, labeled *"in the heart of the Earth"*. The idea of a *"game"* with a purpose came into being. Most of us discovered in the history of the ball game that it originated with the Mesoamerican people as sacred ritual. The ball court frames the cosmos. Performed at special times on the calendar, kingdoms were won and lost on the turn of a game.

> In a legend explaining the conception of the twins, Ixbalamque and Hunab P'u, we hear of a young maiden with a great curiosity to see close up the famous forbidden tree from which hung the heads of the seven ancient lords transformed into gourds. Having tried to convince her father to accompany her, but failing, she went alone. Gazing at the mysterious gourds, the young maiden asks herself: *"What kind of fruits are these*?

Do they have a good flavor? Can I reach one? What will happen if I do?" (These questions are asked when any people discovered new botanical species whose properties they did not know.)

One of the heads speaks, saying: *"What is it that you want? There are only bones hung in these branches. Do you want us?"* Here is the dilemma: the fruit of the calabash tree is not edible; only the bone-like rind is useful."

"I want you," she replies. *"Very well, extend your hand,"* say the heads. The maiden obeys the request immediately. The heads let some drops of saliva fall on the palm of her hand, but when she looks at her palms, they disappear.

"In this saliva that we cast unto you, we have given you our progeny. When we lived, we were handsome, but now only our heads remain from that time when we were great lords. "Since we died, we only frighten everyone", thus, the Maya believe that the knowledge one has is passed on to the children in saliva, whether they are children of Lords, wise ones or orators. Because the saliva is deposited by Lords, the wisdom of the ancestors endures. *"This very thing have we done with you."*

The Maya personify the liquids of Earth: blood, rain, semen and tree sap are equated as divine substances.

The maiden returns at once to her house, impregnated solely by virtue of the saliva. Thus, were conceived the twins, Hunab P'u and Ixbalamque, male and female.

Here is revealed the truth that parents transmit to their offspring intellectual and moral, as well as physical, characteristics. Here the divine origin of the caste of elders is emphasized; its members received their wisdom directly from Deity itself. *Popol Vuh* teaches divine fluid is needed by the Earth—divine fluid correlating with rain, semen, human blood, and the essence of maize all are known as "grace" falling from Heaven to the Earth.

The tree, like the Christian cross, is the symbol of divine martyrdom. The tree receives special reverence as the sustainer of life because of its critical role in the atmospheric rain cycle. A Maya saying is, *"From this tree (the Ceiba [say-ba]) the first human emerged . . . . With the death of the last tree comes the death of the last human."* It is through the family tree that human generations descend——as did the divine twins, who fell into the womb of their mother. The tree engenders the first feelings of property and of native land. Veneration of the sacred tree, human skulls and ancestors begins here.

The story continues: Six months later, the father noting the pregnancy of his daughter, judges it a dishonorable thing—a reflection of the views of the period—-he informs the Great Council. The council unanimously resolves to compel the maiden to reveal the name of her lovers, but she can do no more than tell the truth of what happened, stating only that "*never have I known the face of any man.*" (Maya custom prohibited women, as long as they are single, from looking into the faces of young men. Women were accustomed to turning their backs to the men they met anywhere, and also when they served men anything to eat or drink.)

The father orders her killed; the daughter protests her innocence, restating that she has not transgressed the laws of honor and does not deserve punishment. She proclaims that the life she bears was conceived only because she went to express *"her feelings to the heads"* of the Lords. Faced with the dilemma of carrying out their master's orders and possibly sacrificing an innocent person, the executors vacillate, wondering how they can let her go free and still provide physical proof they had killed her.

Here is a repudiation of human sacrifice. By the proclamation, the virgin separates herself spiritually and materially from the past and presents a new belief for the new cycle.

The maiden suggests they place the sacrificial cup before the tree. Then a red liquid drops from the tree into the cup, where it coagulates like blood and takes the shape of a human heart. The substitute heart is delivered to the Father to be burned. When the council smells the sap and sees the smoke, they realize it is fragrant. The four intended executors become her first servants.

The maiden now presents herself to the mother of the Lords and says, "*Since I am your daughter-in-law, I am your adopted daughter*". But the old woman rejects her saying, "*Who knows where you come from? My sons are dead. Get out.*" The maiden responds, "*It will be proven by the beauty of the countenance of my child.*"

To fulfill the challenges of the sacred writings, the maiden must face tests and teach right-response to life situations. She succeeds wonderfully well; the old grandmother accepts her and promises protection of the babies she will bear. Who she now knows are wise ones. At dawn the maiden gives birth to twins; but the grandmother did not see them born, because they saw the light of day in the woods.

Many teachings are being presented here:
* The solar god comes at dawn . . .
* The early Sun should find us in a Holy place . . .
* The woods are the temple of nature . . .
* Children are best born outside . . . in the sacred woods . . .

In accordance with the mystical conception, the infancy of the twins is lived in a testy atmosphere fraught with dangers. Maturing the hard way, they acquire wisdom and self-control. They demonstrate a wondrous new consciousness: "They were beings with feelings."

This Fourth period begins with the birth of the twins. Hunab P'u and Ixbalamque begin a new division of family labor between men and women. Power moves from matriarchal to patriarchal lines. As the lives of the twins fulfill their goal they meet challenges and overcome them. They then depart Earth, "immediately raising them-selves to Heaven, one to be the Sun and the other the Moon. Instantly, the celestial vault and the face of the earth were illumined; the two lights remained in the heaven."

Since the Maya viewed science as inseparable from spiritual cosmology, they developed ingenious means of interpreting the universal web of causation and applying it to life. They use this cultural knowledge to chart the past and to predict the future.

At the end of the 11th century, scientist Herschel attributed a definite form to the Milky Way. Others calculated it is composed of 100 million stars. They say to cross the Milky Way, one travels 100,000 light years. The Maya knew the Milky Way as the generator of life, and they called it "ge." They related it to science and copied it in all sacred rites. We find stylized versions of the sacred "G" on the pyramids of Uxmal, Yucatan, Mexico, representing the spiraling form of the Milky Way.

Inscriptions say knowledge originates in the Milky Way. The sun of our solar system is the representative of the Milky Way as it channels powerful energies from a distant galactic core toward Earth, influencing our planetary evolution.

The meticulous investigation of the letter "G" means seeking the root of truth. The value of zero "0" is called Ge, and symbolized by the egg, creator of the Universe. "G" is the beginning, the Egg-Creator, the seed from which human life springs; the maker of primitive things, God.

The "G" represents The Beginning. This "ge" or "G" is the symbolic root of sacredness. Wherever figures with dots around a hieroglyph appear, the dots indicate activity, energy, or "g."

The Maya took the symbolic "G" from our universal memory, from the place where we began as seeds. The "g" or zero is highly revered.

It is not unusual for the sacred symbol of G to be depicted on either side of the nose, reminding us of both the breath as life, and the word breathed in from the Source. On the stones we see various zeros and hieroglyphics. The Maya closely relate the zero and the Milky Way. "0" relates to the essence upon which we depend; "G" relates to the Milky and is Sacred to all initiates, and "T" represents the breath by which we sustain ourselves, and by which we are sustained.

The Maya were the first people on earth to give real value to the zero, but their reasoning did not end there. They knew it as the cosmic seed from which springs all life. Sometimes it is a sea shell or a conch shell; it can be animal eggs or testicles or ovaries, even the aura is a "ge"—a cosmic egg.

Here we find four trees oriented toward the cardinal points of the Earth. The word for tree is pronounced "te" (Tay), and its symbol is "T." The symbol shows the relationship to the Creator "teol" (tay-ole), meaning the tree (te) adds to human existence. Maya philosophers associate the tree with "ol," consciousness or spirit. The symbol of "ol" can be shown as "0" to symbolize consciousness. It is located where the energy of spirit consciousness is centered. "Ol" consciousness is a key Maya saying, meaning 'To recall the past is to awaken." Trees are life forms with reactions similar to humans.

Above, the "Cross of Quetzalcoatl" represents the five regions of creation, each with its special tree and color. Red of the East, White of the West, Black of the North, Yellow of the South, Green of the Central position. Though you cannot see a tree in the center, there is, nonetheless a tree there. Each quarter of the creation also represents one of the Four past Worlds. The Fifth World, our world, is the Central position. Note how the Sacred Glyphs surround the Sacred Cross (Fejerrary-Mayer Codex)*

*Shearer, Tony, *Beneath the Moon and Under the Sun* (Sante Fe, NM: Sun Publishing Co., 1975)

Cross of the Quetzalcoatl

Here we see the Cross of Quetzalcoatl or often called the Cross of the Tree. The definition is "the tree that *awakens us*" or *"we awaken in the tree."* It is significant that the tree and the cross were important to the Maya before the Conquistadors arrived. *This drawing is taken from Tony Shearer's Beneath the Moon and Under the Sun, Sante Fe: Sun Publishing Co., 1975.*

"The Table of the Cross," rich in detail, is surprisingly like the cross of Christianity. Many similar symbols—the cross, the tree, the sacrifice, the sacrament of the Eucharist—helped the belief of the Maya to be easily glazed over by the new faith.

Among the Maya, the tree is never associated with evil. It is sacred and connects science, religion and philosophy. It is taught, when the last tree should perish, animals and humans alike would cease to be. The Maya identify with their brother, the sacred tree.

The Maya of Palenque (pahl-in-kay), Mexico, performed rituals in honor of the sacred "T" as symbol of the tree. The temple known as the Palace is one of the sacred sites wherein the Maya worshipped the tree. Often faces of gods/goddesses have a "T" under their noses, symbolizing the divine breath and our relationship to the spirit of the tree.

In Mayan, the pyramid is called "ku," the root word for Hunab K'u. With respect, we kneel in the Presence to awaken our Cosmic Consciousness. We must proceed to live enlightened lives, as the ancient Maya clearly understood.

Maya believe we are all potential Quetzalcoatl's if we but gain the consciousness to realize the status. One can only attain such a state through knowledge of religion, mathematics, astronomy or sciences of the spirit—inherent knowledge.

Teachers, day-keepers or wisdom keepers, will take some persons to train because they are ready and open to spirit. A person should be both intellectually capable and spiritually awakened; as was Hunbatz when he was found by his mentor, then the world is fortunate. The cultures need this kind of help to bridge between traditions.

A comparison to the tradition of the *Bodhisattva or Buddha of Compassion* is present as well. *Hunab P'u*—as the spiritually perfect, illuminated human being—sacrifices himself for the peace of humanity.

The iconology of the young maize god presents us with this symbology. Here is the serene countenance with a crown of maize leaves—the crown, leaves, or thousand petalled lotus of the "*illumined.*" The hands upraised in mudras of blessing: giving and receiving.

The Meditation figure

It is said an individual assumed the lotus posture of meditation to obtain Hunab K'u, the sacred consciousness of native people of Mesoamerica. This position is also, assumed as one puts his or her self into a meditation when wanting to leave the body, or in making attunements with other distant spaces. This is a part of the teachings that are confusing when it is said, "they travel in space." This does not mean traveling in their physical form, but in their astral body. Remarks are made that one could be on another planet in six minutes, (I have heard this said). This in itself does not imply physical space travel, but consciousness travel.

The Maya claim the Greeks came to them. Euclid himself confirms that in 403 B.C. the Greeks incorporated Cara Mayan elements into the still-existent Greek alphabet "Cara Mayan" are two Hebrew words found in the Greek Language that are believed to be originally Mayan. They mean "*peaceful*", "*beautiful*". There is a meditation called "CaraMayan": a pattern of movement set to a prayer or scripture, popular today. In India there are roots of words of the Maya, as there are in Egypt, called "Mayax." The Maya claim "*kundalini*" comes from Hunab K'u and means "*the god spark hidden within.*" The word "yoga" is Mayan, written "yok'hah". It translates "*on top of truth.*"

In iconology, often the central figure of a saint sits in posture, depicted with aura about their head, implying *illumination* or *enlightenment*. Mayan figures are often in the same way surrounded by the sacred symbols of feathers. This knowledge was well understood by the Maya and still is.

Occasionally, a Mayan priest will be shown seated on a pad embellished with planetary symbols. In this way the Maya are consciously reminded to magnify the energy available to be used in health-giving ways. These are shared rather openly and called either *vitality building* exercises or *healing* techniques. One I have enjoyed is very simple and all can do it:

> Stand face to the sun, early in the morning, and speak "Lil . . . Lil" . . . in an elongated manner seven times. Try it and see how energized you feel.

Often, cultural antiquities are symbolized by the deity of Fire. In Mayan tradition, Fire is very old and is worshipped as a symbol of the beginning of human life, as heat. Wise ones are very aware of the responsibility associated with Kundalini.

Many figures of the Maya show powerful resemblance to the Orient. What can be more tranquilly Oriental than a Mayan deity emerging from a lily, as do Eastern deities? In Mayan works of art around A.D. 700-900, we find the "pensive prince" pose of a 7th century Chinese Buddhist as appears often in Asian art as in the book: *Secrets of the Mayan Science/Religion.* Here is a pose of a Mayan figure dating from that period (7th Century).

Also in *Secrets of the Mayan Science/Religion* we find an individual depicted in Arab attire. Many ancient visitors came in the past to study throughout Mesoamerica, says Hunbatz. When the cataclysmic geographic changes occurred, some continents changed and the Maya were isolated for a time. When the Europeans came to the Americas again, they renamed the Americas a "*New World.*"

European culture emphasizes how to live a material existence, but spiritual truth is preserved in the sacred centers of the earth where we conduct sacred ceremonies, say the Maya. We must come to know the seven forces that govern the body to understand their purpose, and understand natural and cosmic law. The Mayan student of consciousness must now use, and understand the movement of the Sun and its governing laws.

In the book, *Secrets of Mayan Science/Religion,* a wonderful concluding chapter is entitled "The Seven Powers to become Quetzalcoatl." It begins, Hunab K'u gave us seven powers and they are distributed in our bodies. The teachings proceed to explain the chakras: "All that exists is only movement and measure in the memory of Hunab K'u."

Most frequently we see the Sculpture of a serpent's head adorned with feathers and planetary symbols representing the teachings and responsibilities of becoming an enlightened person: a feathered serpent. In some we see a carving as at Chichen Inza depicting the head of the initiate in the mouth of the feathered serpent, recognizing the power within each to bring the lower self to the point of new desired awareness . . . that of Holy Consciousness. The Temple of the Initiate is the largest and most important ceremonial structure.

Initiates head in jaws of serpent

Above we see the figure of an enlightened being absorbed by the Feathered-Serpent. This represents the transformation of an awakened one into the enlightened feathered serpent. This carving illustrates the absorption for us. Located at The Temple of the Initiate, and recognizing the power within each to bring the lower self to the point of new desired awareness . . . that of holy consciousness. The Temple of the Initiate is the largest and most important ceremonial structure of Chichen Itza.

Photograph—Temple of the Initiate with initiate in foreground

This 90' pyramid, called the Temple of Kukulcan, is believed to be from the 11th-13th century, built directly upon the foundations of previous temples. This is the location where the inter-play between the Sun and the edges of the stepped terraces create the famous shadow display.

Thus we find embodied in the Maya wisdom:
- The world's most elaborate system of calendars
- A grand style of ritual and ceremony,
- A highly developed language
- An advanced intensive form of agriculture
- A knowledge of geometry and architecture that produced some of the most exquisite temples and pyramids found anywhere in the world

Section III: The Many Worlds of Maya

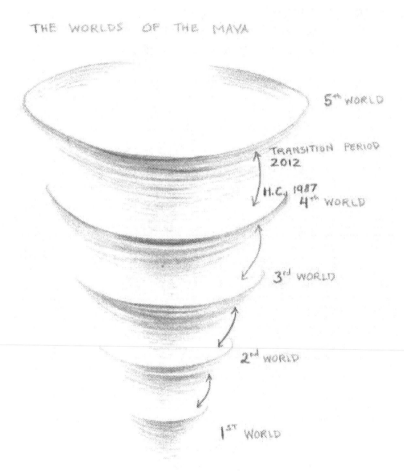

Drawings of the Worlds

A most complicated facet of Maya culture—unique and elaborate—is the system of calendars. They constructed sophisticated astronomical calendars, mathematics and geometry, designed to express the relationship of humanity to the cosmos. Some of the calculations cover millions of years since there are 17 calendars involved, and one has to pick the appropriate one for the purpose being studied, not unlike the ephemeris astrologers use to keep abreast of the movements of planetary bodies.

In the Beginning

About 3113 B.C., Planet Earth entered a galactic wave of 5,000
Years, that ended in 1987. Since then, we have been within the closing part of a great orbit of 26,000 years per cycle, according to Mayan tradition. As we enter the tail of this last 5000-year wave, our planet bounces about in a choppy "sea." Also as we come into this current—this wave—, the bombardment of new energies accelerates.

The further we get into the transitional period, the rougher the current becomes and the more the consciousness of humanity is affected. The Maya predicted Harmonic Convergence would introduce 25 years of challenges, concluding with a grand lift into a new consciousness.

According to the Maya, every 52 years the frequency of human beings shifts. Humanity does not seem to notice these smaller changes but by using the Mayan education we can study the cycles and what they introduce. We must remember technologies do not affect cosmic law, but cosmic law will affect us.

The Dogons, a small North African tribe, were discovered and researched by Sir Robert K. G. Temple in 1967. They lived in Mali, in the former French Sudan. They were in possession of information concerning the system of the star, Sirius, and are mentioned here because they have preserved ancient Egyptian mysteries concerning the importance of the 52-year cycle that most ancient traditions honor. See *The Sirius Mystery* by Temple for further information.

Many ancients used a cycle of 52 year celebrations. We learn from Maya calendars that our solar system takes 26,000 years to make one complete revolution around the star Alcyone, one of the stars of the Pleiades. Astronomers have established that the Pleiades are in effect, a system of Suns that revolve around Alcyone. Oriental astrophysics recognizes, so says Hunbatz, Alcyone as the center of the solar orbit. The German writer, Paul Otto Hesse claims our planetary system forms a part of the systems of suns belonging to the greater system of the Pleiades and that our sun occupies the seventh orbit.

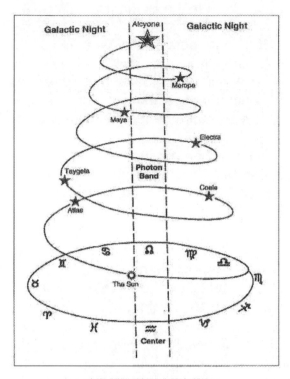

THE ALCYONE SPIRAL

Fifth-dimensional light, originating in the Photon Band, spirals out from the Central Sun, connecting each of her seven children in turn: Merope, Maya, Electra, Taygeta, Coele, Atlas, and finally our Sun. Thus, as our legends reveal, Atlas holds the Earth on its shoulders in space.

© 2003 Harrington,Michael, *Touched by the Dragon's Breath* (Kearney, NE: Morris Publishing, 2003)

Diagram of Alcyone Spiral

The 26,000 year cycle when our solar system circles the Pleiades divides into two 13,000 year periods, one of "light" and one of "darkness". This is not referring to the Sun and daylight as much as it is talking about evolutionary periods of progress or decline. Accordingly, we are now entering a 2000 year time period of evolutionary progress. The cycles of the Pleiades are recognized by the Maya as they figure the galactic alignment we are now approaching. Alcyone is the star around which planet Earth makes its long cycle and we will soon achieve that point.

According to Mayan tradition, for the next 26,000 years this spiral we are entering, called the New World, will see the building of a new civilization. Hunbatz shares, "we must understand our Sun is a part of the Pleiades, and we orbit in concert to the other stars in this constellation. The joint rotation of all the stars in the Pleiades—including our Sun—is but a minor motion within the huge 400 billion—star spiral of our local GALaxy, the Milky Way". The Maya have known about the Milky Way for thousands of years, and they have devised ceremonies to help hold the balance of the GALaxy. Modern science has yet to discover our powerful connection with the Pleiades.

Frequently we see GALaxy as the way the word is written. It is spelled and used in this tradition to show both the respect the chacs want and the importance of the influence, the GALaxy warrants.

The Maya calendar portends big changes ahead: a new age, the *Itza age,* it is called. But before this frequency change is complete, we need to gain the consciousness of Father Sun (in Esoteric Christianity this is the Solar Logos or Christ). We must gain respect for cosmic knowledge. If humanity does not do this, the change will come anyway because no one can stop it. The sun is to awaken everything to greater life. It shines on all of us, not just some.

How will people respond? Some could be very confused by these new frequencies, and according to the Maya, this is the basis for much of the suffering going on today. Other wisdom teachings—certainly Torkom Saraydarian* saw it this way—claim the new incoming cosmic energy as the cause of the rise in crime, violence and mental illness. See *"Cosmic Shocks"*, by Torkom Saraydarian

Right now, the Maya day-keeper counsels: We need to rework our energy bodies so they will be able to cope with the intensifying energy frequencies. One way to strengthen and stabilize the energy body is through chants and mantras (7th Ray, rituals, rosary, etc.) Another important way is through pilgrimages to holy sites around the Earth.

It is my goal to simplify the complex calculations the Mayan Calendar presents. Let's examine the following explanation. Imagine in your mind a complete block of wood with all four sides the exact same length. The length of the piece of wood represents a great, long period of time.

Now, imagine a second block of wood, smaller on all four sides. This block is placed in the center of the larger block, leaving space all around the edges.

Now add a third block even smaller by one inch on all sides. We will continue to add solid blocks until we have nine blocks. On top of these blocks is presented a very small temple.

As you see from the chart above, each block is labeled: cellular, mammalian, anthropoid and then human, etc. These foundational levels represent the collective unconscious as it is developing and covers long periods of time. At the fourth, the human being begins.

The fourth, fifth and sixth levels represent the building of basic self, with its programing and prejudges. At the seventh, world-wide exploration—the planetary awareness-begins as various countries become more and more successful in economic ways. We became rational and materialistic.

The eighth and ninth levels have occurred since Harmonic Convergence and represent the efforts made to build a new conscious. We are now in the ninth level and approaching the October 28th date—John Major Jenkins references as the completion of this ninth level—or December 22, 2012 date as Carl Calleman designates.

These symbolic tiers of blocks of wood construct a pyramid and the small temple on top represents the cosmic egg/seed we are preparing to crack.

We are now in a period of remembrance, recalling the spiritual nature of life and transition, said to culminate in 2011 or 2012, after which we will enter into Year One Katun. The teachings say, after this new katun begins, the destiny of humanity will be guided by the initiates at new schools located at spiritual sites around the world. We might compare this to the ideas about the first sub-ray influence of the Seventh Ray, new age of Aquarius.

More and more initiates /disciples are predicted to collect at *spiritually directed sites* to absorb the wisdom and intensify their dedication, and therefore reforming the modern societies of which we/they are a part.

Recording their knowledge in exotic inscriptions called hieroglyphs, the Maya tell of powerful interactions of the gods and goddesses and the makeup of the cosmos through these carved narratives. They depict calendric and mythical time and cycles, serving as a catalog of important dynastic events, as we shall see.

They state that: A new reign of human enlightenment will commence, according to the prophecies, in the year AD 2013. "If we work with our subconscious, we will then be able to reclaim the information that has been impregnated in the deepest parts of our being! In this way the ancient wisdom will rise again, reminding us of the remote time when humanity was of one mind "and spoke with a single symbolic, mantric and scientific idiom."

Sacred sites, according to Men, remind us to "remember to remember". Their work is to jog our memory. We are to remember, life is for the purpose of a vision quest, or in our language, the path of initiation—that, indeed, we are born to participate in a transformative journey. This inner journey demands our intuition and ability to group-trust and love, much more than just developing an intellectual mind.

Maya teachings offer profound realizations: One does not seek a vision-quest casually; a seeker must be ready to allow life to change, prepare for a rite of passage, and allow movement from one stage of awareness to another.

"For the Maya," Hunbatz teaches as we enter the Itza age, it is "time to give away the knowledge again, to raise the frequency of the global mind. We need to establish a high culture, a new mind . . . a human collective of high principles and high regard for all life". This includes all the kingdoms, the higher world and the lower. The magnetic energy of the Earth and the Cosmos flows more fluidly in sacred sites. When humans make ceremony there, it helps all energy to flow even better.

While there is little agreement between two modern Mayanists, Carl Calleman and John Major Jenkins, as to just what it is that is expected on either October 28, 2011 or December 21/22, 2012, they agree these are both important dates because of the energy that is moving. There is actually no reason to believe life energy is ending. Cycles of energy are shifting and human consciousness is being changed.

The calendars with which we are acquainted are based on measurable mechanical time; this new energy with which we must become acquainted is based on another type of time and energy. We are talking about an energy that is new to us, and after the significant date we will do some adjusting to create a new "steady" kind of frequency.

As we enter the Itza age, it is "time to give away the knowledge, to raise the frequency of the global mind". Hunbatz teaches, "Now the world has a dark civilization, a dark culture, we are to transform our nature and recreate our collective awareness."

Thus, if you have visited sacred sites in any of the honored places, you have already served humanity and the entire Earth plane. This is no reason to stop; indeed, knowing this should cause you to be eager to go and do more such service.

Both John Major Jenkins and Carl Calleman are very knowledgeable and have kept the public well-informed of the importance of the calendar and its challenges. While both are excellently informed on the mysteries and their interpretations, they do not agree as to the important date: either October 28, 2011 or December 21, 2012.

This is good because it helps us avoid getting too fixed on an "end date" as we deal with the Calendar as a lay person. Calendars have used many different astronomical dates over the centuries. Our own calendar, the Gregorian, the Muslin, Buddhist and Jewish all describe measurable mechanic time—Chronos time as it is called in Greek. Modern calendars all use this style based on sun, moon or processional cycles. Astronomical time, because of its base on these planets, will not end in billions of years, so why worry.

Since the Mayan Calendar is based on another type of time than mechanical time, its end date must be discussed against the background of consciousness-based time—shares Carl Calleman. To understand this, we can compare this consciousness shift to a near-death experience, or in a meditation type experience, and not measured by earth time or what is called mechanical time.

Time in consciousness is free floating and is based on an intuitive perception of how grounded consciousness happens to be. In Dr. George Ritchie's, M.D., experience of eleven hours, it seemed hours and hours, perhaps days passed. In my near-death experience, which was seconds and minutes—"short"—I saw myself living in my older years. There is a dis-connect between "inside time and outside time". Understanding the Maya were excellent in using 17 different calendars and then blending them, they came up with dates for measuring the collective consciousness, or at least they seem to have excelled in this system.

The Maya claim they base their calendar on the Tree of Life, and the most respected source is the World Tree at the Temple of Inscriptions in Palenque. This means Mayan time is quantized and describes different quantum states of consciousness based on shifts in time, and not continuously flowing astronomical cycles. We might compare this to an individual making a change or shift when they are internally ready, not because it was a specific day.

The time of various waves of consciousness have been delineated by the best Mayan techniques over the ages and fits a pattern we can call a 9-step pyramid. Each level gets shorter as the steps are climbed. Think this way, as we experience something, it takes less time to make the next conclusion . . . not very technical as far as a way to say it, but it gives us a mental picture of the levels and why each is shorter.

Each is tagged to a certain length, but the length of each differs . . . the main figure of this pyramid is 9 levels high, and each level has 13 measurements to be experienced to make its wave of consciousness ready for the next level. The one place where the end of the world is inscribed is Monument 6 from *Tortugero*. This monument describes the end of the present world as a galactic alignment.

Professional Mayanists say, "We will then witness the display of Bolon Yokte Ku in his full costume and regalia. This is the name of number nine. It means *"Nine-stop", or "Nine-Support"*. To us, we must remember the levels are stages of human growth (of consciousness); each level will last however long it takes the collective to complete that growth; each level is divided into 13 stages, but they differ in time as each one goes faster than the earlier one.

The experts say there is no specific right answer to how this transformation to unity consciousness is to be brought about. While we have tools or techniques, those with active intent will speed up how much progress we can make within each wave of consciousness, and the laggards will present a drag on how high/holy/much Oneness we can reach. Community is still the real one in charge of the event; events outside in other dimensions will try to spur the racers onward.

Paraphrased from The Crystal Skull Guardian Monthly News [md@crystalskulls.com] and http://www.calleman. com/content/articles/risk_of_2012.htm

Said another way, according to Carl Calleman, we are near completion of the final wave of our collective evolution. This wave began on March 9, 2011, just two days before the waves hit Japan. Since the goal is Unity Consciousness, then perhaps traumas such as this achieve their goals or at least a part of it by helping us invoke compassion for our brothers and sisters.

This Ninth Wave is known as the Universal Underworld and includes only a short time in which we are to cap the entire evolution of the universe. The long-promised perfect(ed) being (*homo spiritus*) is to align with all others and become the "*One Son of the Creator Consciousness*". We are to realize that so far our evolving cosmos has been providing these intensifying energy waves from time to time to assist humanity to achieve this Unity. Since 2011 is to be the final wave of achievement, we cannot expect it to be like any other year. This is the crowning glory year for you and me to achieve our goals as a part of the *collective spiritualized* consciousness.

It is taught by those most knowledgeable in the Maya teachings that there is a twenty-fold intensity in the frequency of energy in each wave. The Ninth Wave still has the last few days in which to impact humanity, as they climb the pyramid to be able to witness the appearance of *Bolon Yokte Ku* in "his" full regalia.

If this event is about creating harmony, would not our task be to ask the divine for guidance as to what could we do to arrive at this *Unity? What can I do to serve the cosmic plan?*

There is no right answer to the transformational question. We have to have an honest intention to align with the cosmic plan to let our prayer bear fruit. Also we should remember our perception of the future is very likely to be different than anyone else's. So we are creating parallel futures even as we seek unity. Events must occur to help our *collective futures* merge. Touching and traumatic events cause more empathy to stir as humanity seeks to outgrow its "*separative*" attitude and to gradually let go of its powerful *ego stance*. The Cosmos will keep stirring us to help humanity realize its great goal; that is, its fulfillment of the Great Plan.

The Structure of the Mayan Calendar

Over Simplified yes, but some clarification!

Many of the challenges of the modern world are blamed on separation. The definition of *"separation"* in Maya belief is *"an illusion that causes dis-ease and dis-trust, even of the sacred voice within our-selves."*

76

The Mayan appreciation of Crystal Skulls

The Mayan people have a deep appreciation for crystal skulls as do many other North and South American cultures. Today, modern-day interest is informing us of many interesting effects they have or have had upon the peoples of our continent.

Indigenous people of both North and South America have demonstrated a great respect for Crystal Skulls. Some believe they hold the knowledge of the ancestors, and in attuning to one we achieve a higher frequency and a greater understanding. Some believe they are remnants of the Atlantis culture, and others think they are from outer space. It is thought that they have healing powers, or at least aid us in harmonizing with our higher consciousness.

The stories contain legends about a woman turning into a crystal skull. As you recall, the legend about the virgin conceiving the twins from the skulls hanging on the Ceiba tree, or tree in the center of life. Crystal Woman, popularly known as Crystal Skull, and sometimes called Gentian; functions as a transmitter between the world of supernatural and humans, particularly, medicine people. Native American stories contain legends about Crystal Woman turning into a crystal skull. The story is that the skull is of one who was originally an earth dweller, (b*ut non-human*) and was *"Magically"* transformed by exhausted ritual.

One of the most famous locations from which Crystals Skulls have been found is Lubaantun (loo-bon-toon) in Belize—means "place of fallen stones"—with 11 major structures distributed loosely around five major plazas. It has a regional religious, political, administrative and commercial center.

Lubaantun is best known as the origin of the Crystal Skull, unearthed by the famed F.A. Mitchell-Hedges in1926. The story is that his 17 years old stepdaughter, Anna, spotted something shiny and reflective within a pile of rubbish. Three months later and a short distance away a detachable jaw was discovered and re-united.

It has been publicly shown to many in the United States at Spiritual gatherings and retreats. This well-known skull is said to be the most perfectly formed major crystal skull known presently. The owner, Anna Hedges, has since deceased and the skull has been placed in a museum in London.

There is also a very popular crystal skull in Houston, Texas. This one gave his name as "Max," when it communicated with its new owner, Jo Ann Park. His formal name is *"Texas Crystal Skull"*. He was gifted to Mrs. Parks by a Tibetan Lama after having been on a healing altar for many years. She had served as a secretary to the center for some years before the Tibetan Lama's life ended in 1980. Its history is somewhat unknown, but it is often available for public viewing through a foundation.

On our trips to Maya land, we have met several times with "Max" and had special meditations. Jo Ann is willing to let persons touch him or place their forehead against his. People have had many different reactions . . . very creative. JoAnn and Max have been guests at creativity workshops many places and times; individuals have quite interesting reactions to the skull.

Some say, crystals and crystal skulls can help us raise our vibrations where we have difficulty doing so alone. They have been used by native people world-wide historically to do so and to maintain wellbeing. Quartz is next to the diamond in density and can be used effectively by the average human being that relates to "the stones". There is a long history of healing properties in crystals and gemstones. Likewise, Turquoise, Malecite and Jade have all been used for all-purpose healing by Ancient Egyptians, the Tibetans, the Aztecs as well as Mayans and Native Americans.

In the face of negative situations, do not give in to feelings of fear or powerlessness, but to use whatever tools you have to harness your power and direct your thoughts and intentions to influence your desired outcome. Crystals and Crystal skulls may be able to assist you to do so.

A popular occurrence in Native American gatherings as well as some others is forming a circle of crystal skulls to represent the various groups or tribes that have matured individually. In the center then is placed an exceptionally good/famous/powerful skull to represent the "Collective Group Mind" that we are also building.

Thirteen Crystal Skulls

Maya writings reveal legends about the skulls hanging on the Ceiba tree, or Tree in the Center of Life. These skulls—hanging shiny and bright from the tree—remind me of the Sephiroths on the Tree of Life in Kabalah. Is there a connection? Of course—the Tree of Life is exalted in every tradition.

Elongated Skull

In Peru we learned about *elongated skulls*. It is a custom that provokes lots of conversation as it is a custom found world wise. We had watched the movie of Erich Von Daniken before going to Peru so we visited as many of the sites mentioned as possible. We learned about 1870 these misshapen skulls began to be discovered, and as they attracted attention, they were discovered all around the world.

By the practice of "cranial binding", as it is called, or by various other names, we find skull deformation is found in nearly every continent. Less known in the U.S., persons cannot help but wonder what triggered such a practice. Questions raised are many but specifically, "Were these made to be similar to the elite and made so as a status indicator?" "Were they mimicking an alien race with which they had contact?" Or, "was there a group memory they honored?"

It may be a form of artistic expression such as tattoos, piercings, and ear or lip stretching, even making neck rings to bind and stretch the neck. Humanity has found many ways to express its creativity, and elongating skulls may be one of them.

At Palenque there is much importance given to a teacher. Pacal Votan, one of the most important rulers in South American history speaks of and his appearance shows an elongated skull. Also, we have reason to believe Akhenaton of Egyptian fame had an elongated head as well. Were these natural or created, we have no way of truly knowing? They may very well be a remnant of an earlier alien race that mated with humans and the long shape was inherited for a few generations.

From a text Hunbatz once sent me, we read:
> *"The ancient Mayans worshipped the teacher Pacal Votan for his great wisdom because he was an enlightened one and he knew everything. According to Alberta Ruz Lhuillier's book, some inscriptions in the Temple of the Inscriptions in Palenque say that Pacal Votan was an initiate who had the ability to do healing miracles. He could cure many illnesses just by raising his hands or through a look. Then we can say that he was able to perfectly handle the energy, which he could control and regulate with his body and mind.*

> *"Pacal Votan taught his people the mystery of the 9 BOLON Ti K'U and the 13 OX LAHUN TI K'U. He taught his Mayan people that the 9 BOLON TI K'U are the Lords of the Night and their wisdom and power depend on the absence of light. Also he taught them that the 13 OX LAHUN TI K'U are the Lords of 13 dimensions; he used to say that every initiate should be aware of knowing these 13 dimensions because the explanations to all the existing mysteries in the world, either physically or non-physically, could be found there.*

The ancient Mayan priests of the old times claimed the spirit of Pacal Votan came from the stars and that was why he brought the wisdom of the stars with him and knew the 13 OX LAHUN TI K'u. They also said that after arriving in our Mother Earth, he decided to work with the human beings forever teaching them all the current well-known sciences plus other unknown sciences that are even unknown to us these days. According to the Mayan priests, Pacal Votan knew the tunnels of time.

"When Pacal Votan arrived into this world, he was already enlightened with the wisdom and brought the history of time with him. When he spoke of the ancient times, he showed a figure of the Eocene Era, the time in which the animals we know and still inhabit the planet appeared on the Earth. Then he used to tell his Mayan people that the human race already existed, but they lived in other very distant places called Continents, now these Continents are sunk under the seawaters.

"Pacal Votan had many disciples and many of them traveled to other Mayan temples such as QUIRIGUA AND Copan to share this wisdom; that is why many inscriptions found in these places are similar to those found in Palenque. These days, it is advisable for all the initiates who do initiatic works to go to those places to absorb the teaching found in those Mayan temples of light."

Pacal Votan's picture

Pacal Votan is one historical figure all Mayan hold in the highest esteem. A biographical card from there states re: Por Moises Morales M. (Founder of Palenque's Round Table) tells us that,

"King Pacal was the most important man ever to be known in the Western World history."
He repeats this version regularly, saying:

> *"How in the World could he think that, in Palenque is buried the most important man ever born since the beginning of history? Pacal was crowned by his mother July 29, 615BC; ruled for more than 67 years. But, due to Europe's barbarian occupation; Africa did not develop important cultures, while in America Mayan's are the most evolved culture at that time. Mayan culture was the most important in the hemisphere and Pacal was the most important man.*

> *The drawing of his "Palenquean Head" was found in 1952, under his sarcophagus, which coincides with his physiognomy and the several representations that we know from Pacal, which the hieroglyphs which identify him, is the young Pacal. These show his elongated head* (and on occasion we see him portrayed with extremely long legs)."

There are many drawings of King Pacal, as he was known, and also the famous sarcophagus photo of his tomb. Most construe this drawing to be an "astronaut" but it is considered by Hunbatz to be the meditation position recommended and assumed when one seeks to attune to the cosmos or distant worlds.

Sarcophagus often called the "Astronaut"

King Pacal (also known as Pacal the Great) was born in the year 603 A.D. He was king of the Maya kingdom of Palenque and is said to have reigned for 67 years until his death at the age of 80. The name "Pacal" means "shield" in the Maya language. Pacal expanded Palenque's power in the western part of the Maya states, and initiated a building program at this capital that produced some of the finest art and architecture of the Maya civilization. He was preceded as ruler of Palenque by his mother Lady Zac-Kul as the Palenque dynasty seems to have had Queens only when there was no eligible male heir. Zac-Kul transferred ruler ship to her son upon his official maturity. He ascended the throne at age 12 on 29 July, 615 A.D. After his death, Pacal the Great was worshipped as a God, and said to communicate with his descendants. His elaborate temple tomb had a stairway down to his crypt, and after this was sealed up it had a long "speaking tube" connected to the temple atop the step-pyramid.

Wikipedia www.wikipedia.com

From stone carvings we have proof that for a period of time the Maya had a practice where they attached a bead on the forehead dangling above the eyes to encourage "crossed-eyes" which had some honored status for the child as it became older. In Mayan carvings, the eyes are often shown turned upward, toward the third eye. To these folks, this seems to have become a sign of prestige for later generations. Infants and small children were banded about the head with a bead dangling on the forehead and over the nose to train the eyes to stay in an upward position. Many such reconstructed statues can be seen in Edzna, Mexico, as well as at other places.

While some think of the Maya as bloodthirsty, in traveling within the Maya areas, we found the modern people gentle and humble, proud of their heritage and struggling to preserve native ways. We are told great wars developed between the powerful city-states, and rivalry brought about their destruction. The true story is still emerging as we listen to the wisdom keepers. It is exciting to live in a time of the rise of a great people, for much interest and influence has been generated by their calendar, which fortunately has been preserved for the deliverance of dignity and value to their heritage.

As with other old and noble traditions, royal life was recorded, but lesser details were ignored, along with the problems or imperfections of the rulers. However, highly ritualized lines left an understanding of the patterns and order of the cosmos in the minds of their descendants, which even today engenders a deep connection to spirit reality. Their old ways continue to survive woven into the modern culture.

The Maya believe each kingdom has a work to do, and the work of the human species is to become "*feathered serpents*"—Quetzalcoatl, Christed ones, or illumined beings—as a result of the sacrifice of the Father, Son, and Mother Earth. Remember "sacrifice" means "to make sacred"

I now share a story of the love humanity can have for its brothers and sisters:

On one trip to Guatemala, I found a wonderful, nearly life-size statue in a Christian Church. It was in a small church on Lake Atitlan in a small village of Santiago Atitlan, where the most traditional Maya live, wearing their unique woven tribal patterns and located about one hour from Panajachel with its wonderful textiles. You will see the statue below. First, I must tell you about a divine love that happened here in this little village.

They had a dedicated American priest who had been warned to get out of town. Remember, the revolutionaries in the 1980's who were so fierce? They sought to rid this community of outsiders so no one could report the abuses. He was told to get out several times.

He did not go; he was threatened several times, and then in the middle of a night he was murdered. This is a true story. The priest was from Oklahoma. We loved him for his care of the people and for his courage; so we wanted to visit this particular church in his memory. The priest's name is Father Stanley Francisco "Aplas" Rother. His body was returned to USA minus his heart.

Gravestone for murdered Priest

Arriving there, we said the Aquarian Rosary in his memory. While there, we saw a number of local Guatemalans come, kneel, and pray to him. They would say in a loud whisper, "Padre, Padre, help me" or "help your family." What we learned as a local legend was that when his family came from the U.S. for his body, the Guatemalans did not want to give it back.

They resisted, finally negotiated giving his body to the family that agreed to leave his heart with them. Knowing how much he loved the community of folks he had served and died for, the family allowed his heart to be put in a container placed in a block of concrete. Then installed in the middle aisle of the small church, more or less right in front of the altar, his heart is available to the people when they need him. We saw people kneel and talk, as if he was still there with them . . . and so he is.

The old Spanish priests would be shocked to see how well the natives have fit the old religion and the new together. What we see here shows how well it epitomized the merging of the two.

Inserts: Historical Christian practices still exist among Mayas

Photo of Mayan Altar

Fig 1: *Here we see on a Christian altar a Mayan climbing his way to higher consciousness, carved, and still there for our review. Think of this as humanity climbing to a higher vibration to become the new human.*

Open areas above Altars

Fig 2: *Additionally we see, open areas over and behind the altar as Mayan men who had never worshipped indoors, had some difficulty adjusting to an indoor practice of the Spaniards. Alcoves open to the sun were built in order to persuade men to enter the new places of worship. Women were accustomed to worshipping in caves, under the pyramids, or enclosed areas so they were more accepting. Worshipping in closed buildings was a difficult new experience for the men as was men and women worshipping together.*

Older confessional

Fig 3: *One of the oldest Christian confessionals still in use in Guatemala Cathedral, Guatemala City.*

Confessional with Doors in use as well.

Fig 4: *A later confessional with doors has come into use in some cathedrals.*

As we would say, "*Thanks be to the Son*", the Maya tell us, *"Each one of us has a sun within to salute. As the inner sun radiates its light, the aura bears witness to the sun held within. That sun brightens our aura with more and more of its energy; we become sun beings, bearers of light with a work to do, illuminating our place in the world."*

In Esoteric Christianity we acknowledge the solar deity as the Christ. Christian teachings seek to lift us into a new awareness of the Self within—the hope of glory—to become a part of the mystical body of Christ. To the Maya, the high consciousness is represented by the feathered serpent. To these the symbol represents kundalini (*spiritual power of the awakened Holy Spirit*) moving through the body to unfold what we call the thousand petalled Lotus (*feathers to the Maya*). This idea is presented in the headdress of many historic people—crowns, Viking helmets, and turbans.

Altar showing Father, Son and Holy Ghost

Returning to the statue on the altar: We see a form of a man dressed in the local attire. Looking closely, we see him representing God the Father (seated), depicted as an old man, while on his knees is Christ Jesus (on the cross yet), again, in Maya dress, and with the Dove of the Holy Spirit over the heart. We were amazed to see how clearly this shares the Christian teaching, and so you see the photo above, taken January 1994.

Carol E. Parrish-Harra Ph. D.

To be Acceptable among Those of Expanded Awareness-

*The Wise Ones of antiquity knew that "Sun worship": (which, more accurately, probably was "Sun meditation"), in reality, was the development of a personal relationship with **That** for which the sun stands.*

Thirty-five hundred years ago Amenhotep IV wrote:
"The supreme creator of the universe is the One God, to whom, through the light of the Sun, all eyes and hearts and minds must be directed."

The theosophists, in our century, have explained that behind the physical sun is a spiritual sun, the heart of our universe.

When we think of Hunab K'u, the sun deity, as the Giver of Movement and Measure, we need to hold in mind the symbol for the Creator, a circle as movement placed in the square as measure. The square represents the man, or masculine consciousness; the circle symbolizes woman, or feminine consciousness. So, movement and measure illustrate the world of duality and all that is separate, reminding us that all is coming back together. Whatever is separate needs the other; *All* are to be *One*.

We have now almost completed the last decade of the transition period which began at Harmonic Convergence in 1987. Either by October 28, 2011 or December 21, 2012, we are ending the 9th hell that has changed us vastly during this last twenty-five years.

Humanity has certainly transcended some of its limitations with which it has falsely identified. We now identify with the importance of the kingdoms of nature. Each five-year period carried us more toward the mind of an awakened one. We are more aware of the higher possibilities through technology, scientific research, and education than we were in 1987.

It is as if a lock is placed on humanity at that date (*end—date/change-date*) to measure our '*frequencies*". We will deal with all the negatives from now until then. What we register in negatives will manifest itself in stressful ways during this period to see how much we can purify . . . greed, hostility, racism, warlike behavior, etc. The new cycle will begin at that time with the resulting difficulties blended to the incoming energies as a starting point upon which the New Age will be built. The more pure the "*frequencies*" of the human *heart-mind* at that change-date, the better the "*next-world*" will begin.

The Maya suggest the Earth's fourth-dimensional body is preparing for a galactic culture, and the planet's guiding mechanism is situating itself to make that connection. The Maya believe both *Mother Earth* and humanity are aligning with *Father Sun* for the changes we are approaching. Everything within the Earth's biosphere grows, appears, moves, and transforms does so by attunement to its Crystalline core. This is the basis of geomancy, planetary spiritual sciences, dowsing, and so on, and the basis of Earth telepathy, known in spiritual science as planetary psychometry.

Hunbatz Men says in *Prophecies from Solar Initiation;* someday keepers intuit what is to happen, but only a few can use both the teachings and their inner awakening. When Hunbatz reads the hierographs, he reawakens to the understanding that is preserved. He shares with us most Maya cannot read the teachings, either, so they too, need teachers.

As a result of the changes going on in humanity, we are encountering new cosmic energies, and resonant frequencies are synchronizing in a pattern corresponding to Earth's harmonic grid—so gradually the grid is being amped. Two things are then to occur: 1) simultaneous activation of collective memory patterns to help humans transform, and 2) the manifestation of large-scale atmospheric-energy, spectral phenomena, or energy changes.

Jose Arguelles once said, "*The Campaign for the Earth is the moral equivalent to world war*". If you said in 1940 that the way we're going to end the war is by unleashing the power of the universe, people would have said, "*How are we going to do that?*" Yet, in 1945 we split the atom.

The message was sent throughout the GALaxy, the bonding of subatomic particles of the physical plane had been broken. UFO's began to gather to watch. We are in a position now to do a work called the "*activation of the psi bank.*" Humanity does this by the creation of a resonant frequency signal, and by energizing sacred sites. Now, the energizing of sacred sites is of great importance.

By 2011 or late 2012, we are to be recognizing the Oneness of humanity and our connections with the world of nature that has for so long been seen as mechanical rather than alive and stimulated by sparks of divine life as humans are. General agreement is that these predicted happenings are coming.

We learn the Earth is activating a psi bank. By developing our minds and outer communication, we have linked externally. Simultaneously and inwardly we have been wiring (slowly evolving) a fourth dimensional human body of light. At this crisis point, we hasten the building of this light body, or we will begin to deteriorate. Harmonic Convergence (1987) was a *wake-up call*.

The announcement went out from the Mayan as well as other indigenous sources; around the world groups gathered and celebrated. Specific instructions were given; how to greet the Solar Lord in the morning, and how to say "*thank you*" again at sunset; the creation of a number of days of special meditations, and the importance of creating *joy-filled* events was encouraged.

"*Joy*" best fits the Mayan concept of religion and science, both of which are taken seriously in our culture, with a tendency toward "heavy." Ancient teachings have instructed: "Art, science, and religion can carry humanity back to the same source. Science can get us there, but too often by over-developing the intellect, it gets rigid. Religion may become grief-filled and sad.

Thus, art becomes the less complicated way for most people to touch into archetypes of joy, beauty, and goodness. Sacred writings say the Great Source of Life wishes us to be joy-filled and wise. We are called to celebrate through art, dance, song, chanting, festivals, and play—to be joy-filled.

Broadly speaking, Maya prophecies fall into five categories: day prophecies, one-year prophecies, 20-year prophecies, and special prophecies of great cycles, and the Return of Quetzalcoatl.

Hunab K'u wants individuals to be prepared because sacred scripture has prophesied difficulties lie ahead. Initiates must learn to transform sacred energy in our minds and bodies. When one experiences the sacred moment, when one is imbued with cosmic energy, we know the giver of life. We must reject three dimensional laws and perceive the presence of our parent, the Sun, afterwards then, we will awaken.

Let us begin to examine some of the concepts familiar to the Maya.

Don Pascual, Wise elder of the Mam Maya states, *"When a wise one speaks, it is not to convince the incredulous. They do it to guide and awaken the consciousness of those that follow the path towards consciousness. Their words are not only for intellectual debate or for the nourishment of the spirit. In actuality, the spirituality of these prophetic times, are not limited to contemplation and meditation. Today spirituality is synonymous with action; and action is every act of your life, in harmony with Mother Nature, and most importantly the harmony within ourselves, and in relation to the way in which we live."*

Maya prophecies promise that people of many lands will begin to seek the knowledge of the stones that vibrate with ancient secrets in the Itza Age. Pilgrims will come once again to learn to rediscover the secrets and philosophy of the Maya.

Ancient Maya ideas forewarn against the manipulation of the genes of the human being: *"Do not play with sacred knowledge unless you have understanding, humility and the permission of Spirit."* Humans cannot anticipate the effects of genetic alterations.

Hunbatz reminds us of Einstein, who late in his life regretted the use of some of his scientific theories. He says the word gene comes from Maya *"ge-ne"* (hay-nay) that denotes the sacred spiral of life evident in the double helix of our genes, but also in the form of the Milky Way GALaxy.

He asks, "Who is going to change the frequency of the minds of those who are now working with (restructuring) genes?" It is up to us. When one meditates, life becomes much better, but when many meditate, the power is far greater. We need to work in concert on important issues to change the frequency of people's minds."

The Maya believe group minds can change just as did the Soviet government collapsed. Likewise, the governments of the American continents will change as well. They say our mainstream materialistic culture does not have a lot of time left. Cultures come and go unless they copy the laws of eternity as the Maya have tried to do.

It is prophesied that by this time we should be seeing a transiting civilization take place, from a military state (terrorist) to a de-industrialized, decentralized planetary society, but we know this is not complete, or as changed as it needs to be. We can see the decentralization of the materialistic planetary society has begun. However, we can see decentralization developing and much fear arising. Industrialized nations are in disarray and military forces are being reduced. Currently we are seeing the idea of large governments and political structures being re-examined by a number of countries.

Once again, warned of negative thinking Hunbatz affirms, "*If thousands of people believe in disasters, they will happen—not just because of the thought, but also because those who are ignorant take harsh actions upon the skin of the Earth Mother—cutting trees, pumping out the oil that is the lifeblood of the planet, and setting off bombs. Earth is delicate, like a small child. Most people think they can take everything, including the blood of the Earth (oil). Pollution allows harsh energies to assault the earth, and as people cut trees, the skin of the Earth becomes vulnerable to cosmic energies that penetrate the Earth, leading to further imbalances.*"

A danger sign to alert us is that, by 2013, should we see big white circles in the sky we are to know that it would be an ominous sign that we had failed to make a successful and harmonious transition into the new age, Itza (eet-sa). It is said: "When the world leaders have disorder in their minds, they will throw heat that is enclosed within receptacles." If that comes to pass, it will mean nuclear bombs have gone off, that the nuclear war has started. We can change that. That is also clear from the prophecies. It is possible to change everything.

The Classic Maya of Central America was to create and synchronize the terrestrial calendar cycle with the harmonics of the GALaxy of which we are a part. They are able to do this because of their knowledge of cosmic science—through advanced understanding of time, math, geometry, and ritual. Well versed in binary and parallel intelligence, as well as the science of resonant harmonics, their civilization was actually an experimental research outpost, gathering information for the eventual link-up of planet Earth with a Galactic Federation. Much of this understanding is preserved at Uxmal (oosh-mal): from here comes the idea of some departing because they have returned to their own space.

Once the Maya completed the precise calibrations necessary to put our planet (as a representative of our star system) into phase with the galactic harmonic, the Chief of the Cosmic Emissaries departed. According to the Mayan calendars, this was in A.D. 830. Knowledge left behind, carved in stone, was transmitted by seers, and symbols cloaked in the garb of myth, and the prophecy of the return of Quetzalcoatl, the Feathered Serpent.

Carol E. Parrish-Harra Ph. D.

Following 1987, the stages leading to planetary civilization are to unfold rapidly, says Jose Argüelles, with galactic climax in A.D. 2012. Said another way, the nine hells were periods of great challenge and pain so humanity would begin to seek the way to the light. By then, 2012, it will desire life, light and goodness.

Just as Harmonic Convergence could not have been calculated without computers, the world could not decipher the Maya writings until computers using the binary system came along.

This complicated process keeps the 13-Moon Calendar (Moon/Lunar-female), and also utilizes a 20-day (solar and male) tribal system to blend influences. Individuals celebrating the Full Moons of the annual cycle are already somewhat ahead in this process. The 20-day solar tribal system, then, is a next step for us to develop. Only now does it appear humanity is ready to begin its look at the secrets of time, which have laid waiting, incubating, until science and religion were ready to reunite.

Anniversaries of Harmonic Convergence are calculated like a solar return, to a yearly anniversary; it is the recycling of solar influence. In being receptive to the energy of the offering, we participate by creating possible futures. We perform artistic endeavors, creative work and spiritual festivals. Happy events are recommended, as religions and sciences can too often become heavy and unhopeful. We are to create flows of positive energies to help with the uplift. Remember Nicholas Roerich says: Science, religion and art, each followed to their origin, direct us back to our Source.

Another segment of these festivals of remembrance is to dance counterclockwise "unwind" linear time and rational mind so our right-remembrance of who we are and why we incarnated can surface. It is suggested we are moving from one ornamental framework to another.

We are shifting in consciousness entering, what some call a "Solar Age", this correlates to what Alice Bailey . . . Theosophist and Spiritual writer, founder of the Arcane School, who was first visited in 1919 by Master Djwhal Khul, her spiritual guide; (also called the Tibetan), who dictated the ancient wisdom teachings to her over a thirty-year period. These comprise twenty volumes known as *The Bailey books*) . . . calls "the initiation of humanity into the new era."

We need to remember in the face of severe prophecies that their purpose is to inspire a change of direction—to change the ways we do life—in order to change the outcome.

In the Bailey material, Master Djwhal Khul says:
"The objectives of the Hierarchy can be stated as four in number—the goals the workers have set for themselves:
1. *"To establish, through humanity, an outpost of the consciousness of God in our solar system.*

92

2. *To found upon Earth a powerhouse of such potency and focal point of energy that humanity can be a factor in bringing about changes of a unique nature in planetary life—inducing an interstellar activity.*
3. *To develop a station of light through the 4th kingdom that will serve the seven systems of which ours is only one. The question of light and rays useless to enlarge upon as of yet.*
4. *To set up a magnetic centre in the universe in which the human kingdom and the kingdom of souls will be united or attuned to the point of intense power which will serve the developed lives within the radius of the radiance of the One About Whom Naught Can Be Said. These Sons of god who have passed beyond the work with human kingdom have plans of a still vaster and broader sweep."*

Treatise on the Seven Rays, pp.217-8

Master Djwhal Khul also says: "*The first outpost of the Shamballa Fraternity was the original temple of Ibez, located in the centre of South America. One of its branches was later found in the ancient Maya institutions*". (A *Treatise on White Magic, p. 379).* This was before Atlantis, says Hunbatz.

The Maya identity of science and religion as one and the same thing reminds us to use life force advantageously—if not adventurously—both for self and the community. Today we are learning religion, science, and art each have a distinct manner of describing creation. The Maya believe they are to protect the Earth for her service to the "eggs" or seeds incarnating here. Wise Ones protect life and attempt to teach the less wise. Those who awaken are *to ride the wave home* to the Heart of Heaven.

This makes me think about the elders of the last functioning tribe of pre-Columbian Americas. The Lacandones, ('La-con-dones') consider themselves the enlightened ones—with their roles assigned by oracles. They are related to the Maya and live in the Palenque area. With Hunbatz I met with them twice and saw them becoming more-bold with their message as they lessen in number.

About 1991 they came out of hiding and issued a warning to the younger brothers and sisters that the Earth is being destroyed. A video was made warning humanity. The video appeared on television warning humanity they were destroying the Earth. These elder ones say they have taken care of the "younger brothers" for centuries, but now they cannot undo the damage done by so many and that they are not going to warn the world again.

The tribe has ceased to bear children because they believe that the Earth is too negative to raise more people, so the route they are taking is to warn others of the dangers, to the Earth, if we do not heed their plea. They see humanity as being self—indulgent, not good stewards of the Earth planet they were given to protect. They venture to remind the world that *when the last tree goes, so too will the last human.*

They proclaimed many new illnesses will appear if people do not listen. They said the mother was the sea spirit before anything was; she was memory, the mind within nature. We might say *the basic nature or innate intelligence,* the consciousness within all life.

The Lacandones attune themselves to the Moon and its energies. They meditate upon the Earth as the Great Mother and believe they are her guardians. In return, she provides them nourishment. They ask that all people make offerings to nature. "*Return to nature; remember humanity's connection*" is their plea. They say, if there are twelve holy ones in a place, it can be protected. I asked Hunbatz about this idea, and he agrees that a certain number raising their consciousness can protect themselves and their area.

> *More recently in 1946, a Lacandon Maya, Acasio Chan and Jose Pepe Chamber, led photographer Giles Healey to the ancient ruins of a small city deep in the rain forest of eastern Chiapas. There were rooms of brilliantly colored frescoes picturing hundreds of dancers, musicians, warriors, and court officials. Rumors of such a "temple of paintings" had long existed since the nineteenth century.*
>
> *This treasure trove of paintings has survived since the classic period (ca. A.D., 600-85). Both Sylvanvnus Morley, a Mayanist with the Carnegie Institution of Washington, and J. Eric S. Thompson, the preeminent Maya scholar of the day, believed the ancient Maya were the peaceful people devoted to religious observance and contemplation* . . .* as does Hunbatz Men, who acknowledges some battles between tribes, but not the warlike people of the Aztec who is widely recognized as blood thirsty. *Archaeology, May/June 1997*

Arguelles tells us that after we emerge from the purification phase of this transition period, we will actually prepare for our net step in the evolutionary shift, which of necessity will involve our coming into conscious contact with what we now know as extra-terrestrial intelligence. He affirms human beings are much more capable than they know, and this is part of the big secret the Mayan teachings reveal.

Section IV: Entering the fifth World

It is taught, there are about 21,000 temples, pyramids and sacred centers in Mesoamerica. These centers are to keep the Earth balanced and to assist in uplifting the awareness of all people. The main temple is "The Temple of the Initiation", at Chichin Itza.

At the 1995 (Solar Initiation) spring equinox in Mexico, the Maya announced a 500-year-old prophesy inviting seven chosen emissaries, stating we were Mayan in the past, or would not be so passionate today about the teachings. It may be so, for this culture had stirred my inner nature without prior conscious interest in the subject. My dream awakened me.

In the big announcement of the program all were told **secret** Maya teachings saying that the DNA for the last 26,000 years has been encoded with a *flaw* that ultimately became a source of *de-evolution*. This flaw causes us to believe we are separate from the Divine Source and caused us to evolve our ego-identity. The flaw was required for a cycle, it is said, but now it is time for humankind to awaken to *one mind* with the Divine. Sacred ceremonies are to help reprogram the human DNA in harmony to our *light bodies*. (*We could also think of this as to help synchronize the personality and soul; so soul-infusion can occur more readily.*)

After we emerge from this transition period (2011-2012), we will actually prepare for our next step in the evolutionary shift, which of necessity will involve our coming into conscious contact with what we now know as extra-terrestrial intelligence. Remember: Human beings are not extra-terrestrials but are in truth super terrestrials. They are to be much more capable than they now, and this is the big secret the teachings reveal.

Most Mayanists have suggested that quite likely there are beings and entities in the universe wiser than we are, and each—we and they—have something to offer. New information and right use of it can be of help to all. They believe they have wiser ways to know than our institutional thinking. The scientific/spiritual ideas of the Maya and other Mesoamerican people offer us ideas similar to what our leading thinkers are now discovering.

Those who have led us in an understanding of these concepts—principally Arguelles and Men—suggest we should note the scientific disarray of old ideas. The New Science is seeing the Oneness of life (the web of life) and how all is interlocked.

With the discovery of DNA and the detection of radiation belts (1953), along with the verification in 1964 of tectonic plates (Plato numbered them at 12 and called the Earth a sewn-together ball), the internal dissolution of the current mental house began. All of these discoveries—DNA, radiation belts, tectonic plates, were necessary to bring about the need for a new mental house, a resonant Earth and a one-world concept.

The overall electromagnetic field of the planet is intensified by the bombardment of massive amounts of radar, television, radio and microwave radiation, flashes its increased signals of change through the morphogenetic field.

We have been amping up the planetary grid. In the wake of these impulses came renewed interest in psychic phenomena, UFOs, psychedelic drugs, inter-species communication and ecological concerns. From a spiritual science perspective we have begun shifting to higher vibrations-inwardly and outwardly. And we will find new operational effects and new life there awaiting our discovery.

Indigenous people have offered few teachings about the Sky People and received little attention to these legends. Now, the World is awakening to these ideas in a more favorable way. Maya teachings say at the end of the Fourth World, many space beings of the Two-leggeds will go home as the Great Medicine Wheel turns.

An uncomfortable thought of the Maya is that Five traveling stars with trailing sacred fire (comets) will pass near the sky path of Mother Earth. These Comet-People will provide new-thought-food for the Earth Mother. The Two-leggeds will see through new eyes. The four clan chiefs—the Chacs—of Air, Earth, Water and Fire—will be purified and strengthened by the new type of *medicine* brought by the Star with Tails. The planet will be replenished and will flourish.

This means during the time of the spiral lift, between now and the end/change date, some are ready to leave here and return to spirit. Those who have lost the abilities of limitless creation, they once carried in their nonphysical forms, that want to return to the Great Star Nation can.

Others will perish in the planetary changes to be born again in human forms afterward. Hunbatz suggests that many former Maya are living through-out this solar system. Just as in the past time, there were meetings with the space beings and the Maya; there will be human openness to contact with spacial beings once again. Now, there is little connection with those outside this world because humans do not know how to receive these beings.

Even presently the Earth Mother's new form is being constructed in the consciousness of ourselves as we love and honor her rhythms and cycles. Interestingly, the work of Agni Yoga speaks of Science, Religion and Art as pathways to the Source. Now we have had dreamers: day-keepers, artists, creative thinkers providing, nurturing for the aspirations of us all.

The faithful who remain to create the fifth World here on Earth will be rewarded with new abilities based on positive thought intuition and what the ancients would call *Strong Medicine* to be used for the good of all.

After certain changes occur all five races will act as one mind, one heart, and one family, fulfilling the prophecy of the Fourth world. Time will no longer limit our world; the children of Earth will travel into the spirit world and beyond; the Sky nation and the Earth world will be unified; dream time and the spirit world will be easily accessed by all. Illness or death will no longer be feared among the Two-leggeds or creature beings.

The Rainbow Tribe (All Five Races) will be welcomed by the Stone Tribe (the holders of the Vibrations and Preserved Knowledge) as wholly healed Children of Earth. Awakened to the awareness that each is able to heal through his/her own thoughts, they will use the strength of their own medicine as they remember they are a part of the World of Illumination. The Future beacons each to see the signals of the new beginning. All illusions will be lifted. They will know Illumined humans are to protect life, Earth, and beauty. This is their work; this is our work.

So, peace will settle into the hearts of the All as they go about their daily work—knowing they are connected one to another, and knowing they all serve the same great purpose. For even as the night is coming, they will remember the new day will dawn. Thus, says the Wisdom.

The *"Mayan Factor"* prepares us for entry into the greater galactic community. Claiming we have a love-hate relationship with other intelligent forces, Jose Arguelles suggests, as we learn unconditional love for other humans, we will be able to love more clearly all other kinds of life forms.

Even with the time of the day, the purpose of the leaves can change. Plants can be good for one thing at certain hours and not good for that at another time. When sunshine, at different hours, hits the tree or even plants, its energy and its effect change. This is why someone wanting to know about things natural has to study so much. This is true of all plants and also it is true of people. We are different energy on different days. So say all astrology experts.

Many have suggested quite likely there are beings and entities in the universe wiser than we are, and according to the Maya, they each—we and they—have something to offer. The Maya have no understanding of the concept of evil: "Everything is good. We understand your concept, but it is not Mayan in nature. We see only the energy of the tree, not to say it is good or bad".

Maya believe their ways to know are wiser than our institutional thinking. The scientific/spiritual ideas of the Maya and other Mesoamerican people offer us ideas similar to what Rupert Sheldrake reports in his concept of morphogenetic fields, as well as concepts similar to futurists, such as Hazel Henderson, Robert Theobald, Willis Harmon, the Green Party, and many others in spiritual activities. The World Healing Day, Earth Day and Earth Summit all express underlying beliefs quite similar to the Maya—just in more modern terms.

They identify science and religion as one and the same thing, the Science of Living well, reminding us to use life force advantageously—if not adventurously—for both self and the community. Today we are learning religion, science, and art, each have a particular manner of describing creation. The Maya understood they were to protect the Earth for her service to the "eggs" incarnating here. Wise Ones protect life and attempt to teach the less wise to do so as well. Those who awaken are to *ride the wave home* to the Heart of Heaven.

They meditate upon the Great Mother and believe they are her guardians, and in return she gives them nourishment. They ask that all people make offerings to nature. "Return to nature; remember humanity's connection" is their plea.

Another unique piece of the teachings is that their calendar links the Earth-to-Moon cycle, as well as overlapping cycles when the solar cycles are likewise calculated. Major changes come when the Sun and Moon cycles coincide. Now we are told astrologically we have a series of lunar, solar and zodiacal shifts converging harmonically to synchronize our Earth/Spaceship with the new wave in the four-dimensional mind.

On each anniversary of Harmonic Convergence many have tried to provide a reminder of the trigger event to *re-inspire* themselves and others for the task at hand. Harmonic Convergence was the date which the Earth entered a time of major change—a time of breaking free from the past and of a movement upward on a spiral of evolution. We are moving toward higher vibrations.

The experience has been described, as our planet entering a series of spirals that seeks to draw all that can vibrate to a higher frequency upward toward synchronization with a greater galactic wave which, in fact, will align us with what the Maya call a new world. Most perennial systems have some teachings addressing the close of the age and the beginning of the next.

The polarity response to the dissolving, old mental house was space exploration, the materialistic extension of the acquisition of "*outer space*." The Conquest of Space, as it has been called, began with the Moon-landing on July 17, 1969, followed by probes to Mercury, Venus, Mars, Jupiter, Saturn, and finally on January 24, 1986, Uranus.

Two major findings (though somewhat suppressed) were the so-called "*Face on Mars*" on July 25, 1976, and the highly irregular markings on the "*Uranian Moon, Miranda*", as well as the solar-oriented polar tilt and the discovery of the incredibly intense and erratic electromagnetic field of Uranus.

Immediately following these discoveries, we witnessed the space shuttle Challenger explosion, the technological failure of the next three NASA space launchings, and the explosion of the European space launch Ariane—all between late January and Mid-May of 1986. Many felt we were not being allowed to go into space with a distrustful attitude; perhaps this has or is changing? Or perhaps we now have more willingness to accept, we might just find "*something*".

All of this is the response to our attempt to carry our control issues to outer space. If so, we set off erratic waves of dissonance. On May 23, 1986 we are told 13 UFOs buzzed the Brazilian Air Force. These events become far more important when seen in the light of the decoding of *The Mayan Factor.*

According to legend, *on the terrible night of the fall of the capitol city Tenochtitlan* (**ten-ock-teet-lon),** *to the Spaniards, an omen appeared symbolizing the break-up of their cosmic order:*

> *That night it began to rain—more like heavy dew than rain—when suddenly the sign appeared, burning like fire in the sky. It wheeled in spirals like a whirlwind, showering sparks of light like red hot embers. It rumbled and hissed, like metal on fire. It circled the walls near the lake shore. It hovered over the temple, and then it moved over the middle of the lake, where it vanished. No one cried out when the sign appeared. The people knew what it meant, and they watched in silence. They knew their great civilization was dead. It is believed by most, in rereading this data today, the omen was a spaceship.*

Another concept important for us to realize is that *terrestrials* are not really *aliens*, only more subtle life forms of our planet that we have not comfortably accessed. As the planet is lifted into a new dimension, this new life reveals itself more openly. We eagerly await discovery of our solar system neighbors, as well as the parallel kingdoms of our planet.

In *Agharta*, as earlier introduced, we find new and different societies exposed; we have these materials by Raymond Bernard and others agreeing with such ideas as hollow earth, inner earth, and special societies. (The Smoky God by Willis George Emerson, The Missing Diary of Admiral Richard E. Byrd, International Society for a Complete Earth (ISCE) Danny L. Weiss P.O. Box 890 Felton, CA 05018).

Jose Trigueirinho has some most interesting concepts also and offered a great deal of material on special beings and inner earth systems etc. Different individuals have written much about these other realities. As Mayan people believed we find no end to the many life forms and dimensions where life can be found.

The Interpretation of sacred symbols varies because of the multiplicity of meanings offered. Different ways have been perceived by the different cultures and time frames of various people. The name of the tree is *Te* meaning "*life*"; reversed it is *ET,* or "*brother.*" I wonder: is it a coincidence we call the space beings "*ETs*"? Mayan teachings offer, we are just as much the brothers of trees and other Earth forms as we are brother to the beings of space.

The discomfort we experience when we study and talk about *"alien"* or *"spiritual"* topics is caused by fear and our clinging to the third dimension. Not only are we speaking of expansion of the realities now, we are talking of using our subtle senses in new ways as our reality shifts. Already "new" children are attracting attention. We are more accepting of psychic children and of psychic qualities within these children, and with our own experiences.

The Maya tablets suggest all of this; plus other shattering, thought-provoking events demonstrate that not only the roof but the walls as well of the current mental house are crumbling. All that remains now to be reworked is the foundation, the reasoning of modern science that continues to assert the superiority of human intelligence in the universe. Rupert Sheldrake, the scientist, has written a book, *The Physics of Angels*, jointly with Matthew Fox. As we enter the new era, we will see more unity between science and religion.

The establishment of this new mental house is the reason for the many changes we are undergoing. The infrastructure of a new mental house is also making itself felt—a kind of global conglomerate is forming. As increased numbers are awakening, this creates a global brain. Human reaction to Harmonic Convergence sent a signal to the planet and to the universe that we were able to awaken and join together; thus, humanity sent a signal at an agreed-upon time and for an agreed-upon purpose. With eleven days of ritual at Sparrow Hawk Village, we acknowledged our awareness of our part of the plan and joined in *the Salute to the Solar Deity*. A never-to-be forgotten event at Sparrow Hawk Village welcomed Harmonic Convergence with Hope and Joy.

It is recommended that one of the things we can each do to assist healthy change for our planet is to do our own rituals of fasting, purification (in 11 or 12-day segments) as we approach the October 28th, 2011 date and/or December 21, 2012. This shows concern and respect for the forth-coming Galactic Alignment. It is even more effective if done in groups: *"two or three are gathered together in my name"*.

Human acknowledgement of this significant event triggered an acceleration of the harmonic wave of history as humanity speeds into a time of unprecedented synchronization. From then until now, we have continued to have one high energy bombardment after another, usually two or three times a year. Whether many admit it or not, each one is lifting humanity and our planet into new and different frequencies. We can think of this as stair-steps we are climbing in this manner. Humanity is constructing a new awareness of Life in expanding dimensions.

A more detailed breakdown of the 25-year shift can be achieved by regarding each of five 5-year periods as a stage of the death and dying process. It is true the old is dying.

- We are transiting through a closing period. The first five years (1987-92) were a period of denial.

- The next five years (1992-1997) proved more challenging. We can call it anger or passion. Here suppressed emotion broke loose.

- During (1997-2002) things got better after 1997 as we shifted into the third period, bargaining, and began to create some new structures and/or awareness.

- (2002-2007) we faced our most obvious doubts, esoterically we could say "our Dweller on the Threshold". This period is called Depression.

- With much change and some eagerness, we look forward to (2011 or 2012). We know we can do it even as we struggle to stretch excitedly into our dynamic potential. (2007-2012) is the fifth period: of Acceptance.

A Dying Era

The political struggles and financial ones are but the difficulties of a dying system. The bank scandals, business failures, disgusting bonuses, disregard for the middle class, are all indicators of insensitive materialistic greed. In this ninth hell, as is indicated, we are seeing how sick we are. We are all waiting and hoping as we await the shift of consciousness that is emerging, whether actually in 2011 or 2012, the change of mindset is coming. The weather, it has been suggested, represents the emotional nature of humanity . . . it is rough all over the country . . . I might should say the world. Perhaps we will come to be more respectful of the weather devas or we might say the "*chacs*".

We await the vibrational frequency of the Earth grid to shift. This is the basis for the concept that if the collective mind shifts, there will be no physical polar shift. If our minds experience a unifying matrix, as it has been suggested, possible to be brought about by the blending of the senses, impacted by light-sound sensory experience—we will re-stabilize.

Here is the beginning of the new foundation for our new mental house. We will stabilize our own new world, and the old will continue to fall away. If this be so, it is much like someone almost falling down, but catching him/herself, a stumble, not quite a fall. This unsettled period will last for some years as the new consciousness builds a new structure.

The fallacies of the old system will continue to become apparent, but the new has already begun to build and is also becoming stronger. The old technology will continue to age; the new will accelerate into place. Formulated on the concept of cleansing and purification, this activity will be the single driving force as the first few years after A.D. 2011—2012 are experienced.

The pre-and the post-technological formula defining history, DNA is the transformational matrix holding together the primordial and synthesizing phases of radiant and crystalline energy activation. This model (called the 26-unit Tzolk'in or the "keyboard") describes the pattern of infrastructure—not only of DNA but of the universal light body. Without activation of the two-way flow during the passage through the beam in which we are currently traveling, humanity fails to reach its goal.

The major work of humanity during this period is to craft a planetary light body. We are learning our own powers and even how to care for the planet itself. In other words, just as the chief feature of DNA is a double-helix pattern by which a field is created for the crossing-over of information from either molecular strand to the other, the *Loom of the Maya pattern* can be envisioned as a crossing over of two symmetrical flows to either side of the mystic central column, comprising the pattern of galactic activation.

The "*keyboard*" is a genetic matrix of transformation unifying 12 fields of post-genetic radiance of galactic unfolding. The 13th field is, of course, at the center and represents the DNA.
This divine design is of major historical significance. Many perennial traditions have some mystery tradition of 12 gathering about a thirteenth, or core, of great importance.

Certainly we remember the twelve celestial hierarchies assisting the solar deity and pouring forth the blessings upon the Earth. This whole understanding adds significance to both full Moon and Sun festival attunements we practice. We might remember as well, the ancient practice of placing 12 crystal skulls in a circle to represent various group awareness with One in the center to represent humanity's unified consciousness.

A planetary stirring of kundalini has begun. The creating of a planetary shift is the result of the collective kundalini experience well—grounded and responded to wisely. This two-way flow is the Zuvuya (zoo-voo-ya), and it is moving us back to Hunab K'u, the galactic core. Here, collectively, humanity transforms into Quetzalcoatl, the "Feathered Serpent or we could say, the Holy Consciousness, or the consciousness of the Christos is realized.

We must remember that what we are calling the history in this modern period of Maya is a period of 5,125 years (between 3113 B.C. and A.D. 2012); they, however, think in a much longer period. Our work during this period of time is to become one people, one collective.

We are now a part of the planetary message left by the Maya, who tell us both Venus and Mars are closely associated with Quetzalcoatl (ketzalkwatl). When asked if the discovery of the face of Mars is significant to the Maya, Hunbatz says, "It would seem so." As scientists reacted to the satellite photos, so did Maya translators.

It is believed these signs were left so that if we found them, it would mean we were "getting warm"—getting ready to let go of the old scientific models and make the leap in consciousness necessary to rework, balance and synthesize into the new *"mental room"*. We would become aware of our part in the GALaxy.

The message is that the space-knowers, the Wise Ones of the Maya, would return during this significant period of transition, 1987-2012. The last year is designated as 13 AHAU (a-how), the most exalted number—sign of Solar Mastery. There is also the suggestion that, if we unified in significant numbers on Harmonic Convergence, Armageddon would be eliminated and the old mental house would dissolve without total destruction.

It adds that 144,000 units are needed for Harmonic Convergence to be achieved. Ancient people had ceramic coils as batteries. The word *"unit"* can be translated *"coil."* Think of this as a circle of meditators generating a power, or vibration, together—working as a unit—ascending/lifting the group into higher consciousness. Harmonic Convergence was said to have been celebrated by at least 600,000 people joining in meditation and celebration, many more than estimated to be needed by translators of the prophecies, or so it is believed.

In turn, significant participation was to activate the long-dormant archetypal memories and impressions, and with the descent of the new mental house, these "re-tuning" memories and impressions will saturate the mind-field and create an impulse toward new order and evolving new spiritual lifestyles.

The chief feature of these return memories is the theme of *"return"* itself. Not just the return of the Christ or Quetzalcoatl, but the return of the consciousness of all gods and goddesses, heroes and heroines that have always been a part of the human imagination. Quetzalcoatl is the enlightened state, the kundalini energy soaring to the crown chakra.

The Feathered Serpent lives as a potentiality, a seed, within each one of us. Myth will be restored and imagination will be recognized as the great and wondrous power of creation. This collective stirring, a planetary kundalini experience, is a way to explain the return of the Feathered Serpent. We now also know that such an experience lifts and changes our awareness, activates new energy and sensitizes one to surroundings, as well as to spiritual promptings.

Through imagination, the image-making mechanism, we tap into a great energy—a power-to-do. Its impulses can be organized to create break-throughs, solve problems, be happy, to share and to live life as a god or goddess, a son or daughter, or even a co-worker—of the One God. The return is actually to bring to consciousness what has always been stored within us, and at the same time, provides an increase in know-how.

Currently we are seeing the signs of planetary changes: weather, hot and cold, and water, drought and floods, fires and unseasonable temperatures, earthquakes, road slides, large and small, tornadoes and hurricanes, all have made their selves felt. The activation of the ring of fire from South America Northward has begun, and the energy once invested in the Himalayas now moves to the Andes.

A spiritual teacher, Jose Trigueirinho of Brazil, has written numerous books on ancient wisdom and the awakening feminine centers in South America. His work is little known as of present, but rapidly spreading. He enumerates seven planetary centers now becoming active to affect human kind in the future as the chakra system expands to become more active in the more subtle worlds. Planetary centers he names will receive direct impulses emanating from the Planetary Logos, Solar Logos, or even wider Cosmic sources. See *Calling Humanity* by Jose Trigueirinho in English, Spanish and Portuguese.

The Mayan Factor introduces the idea that Harmonic Convergence is to stabilize the world. Like a gyroscope going into a temporary wobble, we will continue to be challenged, but Earth will be moving toward a new alignment to cosmic realities.

In discussing these matters with Hunbatz, he emphatically stated:
"It will happen. There is no question, it will happen—just as cosmic order dictated the end of the Soviet Union." He continued, "So too the end of the way humanity has been. We are the memory of the Cosmos. The memory of the seven planes is awakening and going to change. How are we going to collect our memories to the wisdom of the Cosmos? I could say, but I can't. You must accept what I say. Every time before giving the teachings, look to the sky and call down the memory to help you. We are attuned to the Cosmos, and we will remember our nature and divine purpose."

Our planet will be activated increasingly by archetypal characters, humans playing out impressions revitalized by galactic frequencies. Many humans will come to know they are fulfilling various archetypal memories of meaningful myths, i.e., the Round Table of King Arthur, the Kingdom of Shamballa. The archetypal resonance calls for a circle, a Round Table of 12 knights and a king—the magic of 13 makes itself felt. Avalon is Earth, and the kingdom is our conscious, resonant stewardship of Earth. As a clan pledged to warriorhood, the Knights of the Round Table will be reborn—wondrously clean and clear, ready to mobilize and sacrifice on behalf of those caught on Earth and the cause of Light.

While the Round Table recapitulates the Maya 13, the myth of Shamballa, the mystic kingdom of central Asia is also an echo of the lords of galactic destiny, or the Maya Lords of Time. The kingdom of Shamballa itself is the ninth and central feature in a valley, surrounded by eight great mountains. Its inhabitants attained to a condition of collective enlightenment—inspired by the teachings of the Kalachakra Tantra (the Wheel of Time) received through their priest-kings.

Nine is the number of Quetzalcoatl, indicating both a deepening and a heightening of the seven chakras (energy centers), a unifying of dualities, primal and celestial. The Mayans are similar to the Pythagoreans in their love and respect for numbers. Using **9** as a building block for the re-webbing of sacred sites will create the mandala of our planetary ceremonial. We may think of **9** as completion of the age/stage. When the celebrant blesses and acknowledges the eight directions, he or she then uses his/her body as the grounding point and becomes the nine; it is realized.

Remember, the "*Cross of Quetzalcoatl*" which represents the five regions of creation, with Green in the Central position, and this space is our space. Each quarter of the creation also represents one of the Four past Worlds. The Fifth World, our world, is the Central position. Sacred Glyphs surround the Sacred Cross just as humanity's new consciousness will be a sacred one and influence all the Worlds

As a ritualist making the cross of four directions, the individual wears green and takes the central position. He/she is making the cross of Quetzalcoatl, representing the Four Seasons, or the Four Directions, the cross of time and space, spirit and matter.

The cross of Quetzalcoatl also represents 12 times 12 is **144**, the harmonic light, correlates to the 144,000 that will facilitate the Great Awakening. According to the ancient Maya, god and Mathematics are One. Through activating the proper formulas, we are able to experience our divinity. Please note, 1+4+4=9, or 9 once again is the number of Quetzalcoatl.

The teachings say the return is a promise to help rid the world of the scourge of the Three Lords of Materialism: the false beliefs or illusions that 1) time is money, 2) job loss causes fear and 3) no one has enough. These three lies hold modern man and woman in a limiting state of consciousness.

The truth is "*time is money*" is responded to as "*no, it is not, it is your life*". Your physical life is passing with each hour and is more valuable than money.

"*Job loss causes fear*" but job loss can be seen another way, it is a way to have freedom from what you were doing and to give you a chance to gain new opportunity.

"*No one has enough*" may seem true at one point, but it is not consistently so, there are plenty of situations where "*too much of everything challenges us*".

The purpose of the return is to re-establish the balance between the masculine earth energies and the incoming divine feminine energies. Each of these archetypal variations is strung like beads of insight upon the Maya keyboard.

The return, or collective awakening, is to free us from cultural trance. Though at first we do not appear to be Maya, by the time these events come to pass, and we reach the moment of galactic synchronization, our lives will be in every regard a model of the lifestyles of the Maya who have preceded us.

Only, we shall find ourselves as planetary Maya with a brilliantly simple and yet sophisticated technology based on matching solar and psychic frequencies that harmonize the ratio of the sensory fields and the Cosmos. We shall create a non-polluting technology and live comfortably in small bioregional groups, strung together as information nodes in a communication system without wires. We shall collectively come to respect each other, one another's myths, religions and art forms.

In other words, technology and human consciousness will have been transformed and we will learn to work together. The information now abiding within us will be available, and we will come to understand our new bio-electromagnetic light bodies—individually and collectively. So we ourselves are the path beyond technology.

The mythic name of the fifth dimensional planetary realm of solar lords—the AHAU KINES, custodians of the archetypes of the evolutionary cycle—reconciles perfectly with none other than the Lords of Shamballa. Directly interfacing with the Galactic Federation, positioned in relation to the north magnetic pole of the planet, and in particular attunement with Orion and Arcturus, the Kingdom of Shamballa (where the will of God is known) entered the third and fourth dimensions during one particular stage of the present world cycle.

Arguelles says this manifestation corresponded to a time following the birth of Lord Buddha (born to Queen Maya at 6.10.0.0.0, midpoint of the Long Wave) when the King of Shamballa requested that Buddha give the teachings of the *Wheel of Time, Kalachakra*. These teachings were brought to the Kingdom and flourished under the reigns of seven great dharma kings. After the reign of the seventh, actually a queen, Vivvamati, the Kingdom returned to the inter-dimensional realm, where it remains to the present moment—pregnant with spiritual warriors ready to rain upon the deserts of our modern day. We might call these the Masters ready to return, "*Disciples, ready to return*", or even, Messengers or Walk-ins.

In the meantime, the AHAU (ah-how) KINES, the *Lords of the Sun* have remained in charge and attuned to humanity's evolution. With their assistance and wisdom from time to time, they release electromagnetic seeds called *Archetypes* through the religions of the Sun for the benefit of guiding humanity. In this last cycle (5200 years), the planetary solar cult was the principal means of mobilization of social energy.

From the time of the cult of the *Solar Lord RA in Egypt*, we have been becoming increasingly attuned to solar energy or the energy of the consciousness of the Solar Lord, the Planetary Christ of Esoteric Christianity—Teacher of angels and of humanity.

The purpose of this Solar Lord is to pierce like a ray of pure light at the initiation of the cycle a constant memory of higher purpose. As materialism entrapped the minds of humanity, they became limited to 3-dimensional reality, and the influence of light diminished. The avatars have come for the purpose of keeping light alive—said in Maya language, *"the evolutionary memory alive."* But by the time of the Spanish conquest of Maya in A.D. 1697, the eclipse was total. Enter the Age of Materialism (now for Mesoamerica, as well as for Europe)!

Mythically, humanity's turning to technology and industrialism, rather than our inner guiding light, is surrendering to the force of darkness, called by the ancient Mexicans *"Tezcatlipoca"* (tays-cot-lee-poka) the *Dark Lord of Time*, or *Smoking Mirror*. Thus, we *see through the glass darkly.*

The 25 year period just ending is ruled by the 13 AHAU (ah-how), so we can anticipate a period of strong spiritual rejuvenation. This coming age is to be a genuine planetary golden age if we achieve the great work of our times. So at Harmonic convergence, you and I imaged the highest and best picture we could. Now we await its manifestation.

In *Agni Yoga* we say: When discipline is not regarded as chains, but turns into the joy of responsibility, the *first gate* opens. When cooperation with the far-off worlds is realized, the *second gate* opens. When the foundation of evolution is understood, the bolts fall from the *third gate.* When the supremacy of the densified astral body is realized, the *fourth gate* unlocks. This is the light body of which the Maya prophecies speak

The Maya called the etheric form the *"dream body,* (similarly as do the Aborigines of Australia) because it is the method of travel behind the veil of sleep. They realized this was the vehicle that was in touch with the other dimensions, not limited to the physical.

- The key to our flowering at this present marvelous final stage in our evolutionary cycle lies in the simplicity of being in resonance. We must nourish the light body to repair its circuits, and synchronize with each other.

- First we must find those with whom we can work, pray and play, and then begin to network, link up and communicate—inwardly as well as outwardly.

- Secondly, we must get into position with others of like-mindedness and move about until we find our group.

Thirdly, once found, we must link up and support one another to keep the grid amped with and for each other.

We find this prophecy in *The Mayan Factor:*

> *While I have described the general scientific aspects of the new Solar Age, it is also necessary to consider the spiritual creative lifestyle that will be mobilized through application of the new psycho-solar resonant field technology.*
>
> *Indeed, without spiritual creative foundations, the new Solar Age would flounder and become another abuse of cleverness.*

We must hear the message of all traditions and find the similarities that remind us that what have been heights reached and demonstrated by shamans, yogis and spiritual masters are everyone's evolutionary birthright. We must connect inwardly with our essence and allow it to express.

We must clear ourselves of conditioning that short circuits this natural flow and erect houses of spiritual perspectives, sound, perfume, taste, color—all within the framework of great beauty in our everyday human lives. We must rediscover the art of harmonious living.

There is a coming fleet of ideas, materials, new ideas and new realities. We are coming *AWAKE*! The idea of entering the Photon Band while fearful to some, I believe, is an exposure our planet is receiving of intense light. Teachings tell us that roughly every thirteen thousand years this occurs for our planet, and we experience a high civilization.

An interesting book, *Touched by the Dragon's Breath (A Native American teaching)*, by Michael Harrington, to which we have already been introduced, has a powerful chapter 10 that illustrates for us the fifth dimensional light of Alcyone, that our Sun will be passing through. This is the Galactic Alignment we are approaching. Remember our chart of the Pleiades and introduction of Alcyone (Page 154) with its significance.

On page 149 of this same book, "*in an article outlining the effects of entering the Photon Belt, Dr. Noel Huntley, postulates, 3-5 days of darkness, if our sun crosses the Golden Threshold first. His website, "Duality and Beyond," explores parallel universes, star gates, ascension, and a splitting of reality.*"

Dr. Huntley claims that, "*confirmation of the Photon Band's existence came from astronomers in 1961 through satellite instrumentation. In the early 1980's a radio announcement in the U.S. stated that our solar system was going to collide with an "electromagnetic cloud" in the not too distant future. Follow-up data was suppressed. Dr. Huntley goes on to say that our solar system skimmed the belt for a few days in 1987. Earth is not expected to fully enter until the year 2012. At that time we will experience the full-blown effects.*"

"Photon energy is the result of the collusion of electrons and positrons. Their mass is converted into radiation-protons. After 2012, those presently in control will be unable to suppress this new source of free energy. Healing will begin on a personal level, as well as on a planetary scale."

"This cosmic encounter will result in the uprooting of deep-seated psychological, emotional, and physical diseases. Old patterns will rise to the surface, and will be passed off. DNA will be upgraded by these new, powerful frequencies. Matter will also be affected by intense photon activity. All objects will appear to fluoresce. Dr. Huntley asserts that this great transformation is the much-heralded "ascension," or "rapture.""

"According to Dr. Huntley, there will be a dividing of the way, a splitting of reality. After entering the Photon Belt, there will be a 3rd density Earth and a more evolved 4th density of Earth. This split will not be perceived physically. The "new Earth" is apparently unoccupied, except for a few animals that have recently left and are waiting for us. Huntley goes on to say that, sadly, some families will be split up. Some individuals will go with the 4th density Earth, while others will stay behind." (Ending on Page 150)

There is a story on page 150 that once again mentions 2012:

"In the corner of a little known churchyard in the small Basque coastal town of Hendaye, Spain, sits a battered and neglected 300 year-old cross, a monument to the end of time. The faded Greek cross at Hendaye bears Latin inscriptions that are said to reveal the end point of time."

"The symbolism of the cross reveals a season of destruction from summer solstice to winter solstice over a 20-year period (1992-2012), by pointing to its mid-point, the fall equinox of 2002, when the planetary and solar alignments form a right-angled cross between our system's angular momentum and the galactic center. This date coincides with the mid-point of the past Mayan katun, calculated from the summer solstice of 1992 to the winter solstice of 2012."

"The mid-point of this destructive period foretold by the Hendaye cross falls on September 22, 2002. It is bracketed by celestial events on the solstice, the most prominent of which is the helical rising of the sun and the galactic center on the winter solstice of 2012. As this is the end date of both the Mayan calendar and the Tibetan Kalachakra, its significance becomes even more profound."

"Astrologically on December 21, 2012, the sun will rise in perfect alignment with the center of the galaxy on the cusp of Scorpio/Sagittarius while the moon sets on the cusp of Gemini/Taurus. On the summer solstice at the beginning of the twenty-year season of destruction, the moon was conjunct the center of the galaxy and the sun was in opposition. On the winter solstice, the end point, the sun will be conjunct the galactic center, and the

moon will be in opposition. Thus the solstice alignments, as revealed on the Hendaye monument, act as book ends to our mid-point of September 22, 2002, defining a 20-year season ending in 2012."
(Ending page151 Touched by the Dragon's Breath)

We must remember we are synchronizing a planetary exo-nervous system. What does this mean? An external mechanism that will connect us to one another so that we realize we are ONE in the *"External world"* meaning the physical dimension. Once realized, this opens us to telepathy. All humans will discover they have the natural ability. We will feel with each other in the Oneness; we will operate as cells in the mystical body of Christ. This is why we seek our group or right work. Some of us are living cells of the lungs, some brain cells, some liver cells, etc. How can this be that we are wired to be telepathic beings?

Geobiologist Joseph Kirschink of the California Institute of Technology has found microscopic magnetic crystals in the human brain that he believes can explain the link between cancer and electromagnetic fields as produced by power lines and electric appliances. The average human brain contains about 7 billion of these microscopic magnets, each weighing a total of one-millionth of an ounce, Human beings are naturally equipped to receive and respond to subtle electromagnetic and other waves.

John White, editor, educator in consciousness research and para-science, and author of *Pole Shift*, explores the neuroscience of the brain and its remarkable *"electromagnetic capability"* in his newest book, *The Meeting of Science and Spirit—Guidelines for a New Age.*

Now, we can understand the activation of the psi bank that is in progress. Humanity, as the mind of the planet, is being amped. This explains:
- Illumination
- The 100th-monkey concept
- Each one making a difference
- The mystical body of Christ
- We can add to this list the *cosmic egg*
- Unity Consciousness

The Maya say that this is the closing of a great cycle—but we are also told it is the closing of the evolutionary interim called *Homo sapiens*. That at the close of this cycle, it will be as if a switch were thrown and a great voltage will race through a synchronized and integrated circuit called humanity. The earth's group mind will be in place—the harness or network of wiring complete—and Earth will be illuminated, a sacred planet.

I asked Hunbatz Men about the concept of our planet becoming a sacred planet, and he said that to the Maya it is already sacred—all life is sacred. It cannot be otherwise, but it is our limitation that does not know this. A current will race across the sky connecting the poles, and in a flash of light an iridescent rainbow will witness to the collective mind of humanity. Indeed, we may say in the Maya way: *In Lak' ech,* meaning *"I am another thyself"*, or as a Christian: *"The Christ in me greets the Christ in you."* Or, we could remember the popular *"Namaste"* in Hindi.

SUMMARY OF THE GREAT PLAN

It is apparent that a new era is dawning that is to be distinctly different from the industrial era, just as it was distinctly different from the agricultural era. We are mobilizing to become an ascending world, one people in conscious contact. We now must ask ourselves: Are we the people who have *"eyes with which to see? . . . and ears with which to hear?"*

The story of the *Popol Vuh* tells of the initiatory trials and triumphs of the redeemer-twins; the paradigm of Every Ones' experience on the path of illumination. It sets forth the Maya perception of the ethical mission of the individual and the human community as a whole. As one awakens the spiritual forces within and the serpentine energy vibrates through the etheric body, one reconstructs the individualized feathered serpent. The feathers on the head correlate with the Eastern idea of the 1,000-petaled lotus.

Quetzalcoatl, the feathered serpent of the Mayas, is one with the legendary phoenix. Many stories developed around this figure of the god-man. One stated he was chaste until tempted by evil companions. Then he became drunk and committed a carnal act. As an example to others, he punished himself by renouncing his kingdom and dying by fire. Although his body burned in the flames, his heart was transformed into Venus, the planet of love.

Quetzalcoatl taught his people the need for compassion, humility and purification. The idea of "twinness" was associated with him—this can be his duality perhaps, he and his shadow self, Tezcatlipoca, (or the bringing together the male and female energies within oneself). When he is depicted as Venus, he is spirit; and when he is the dog, Xolotl (sho-lotle), he is matter (note that dog is the reverse spelling of god). The giver of breath, which sets into motion the matter in which lie the seed of spirit. This spirit awaits his breath in order that it might be born as light or consciousness.

And, is the phoenix one with the thunderbird of the American Indian, which was said to live above the clouds? It seems the plumed serpent, the thunderbird and the phoenix can all be representing one and the same Divine Spirit.

Myths tell the story of the previous worlds, or ages, of the Mesoamerican people. As this information is of heightened interest at this time, here is a simplified summary of the worlds, or ages, according to Maya myths.

In the **first age**, water reigned supreme until at last it rose and swallowed all creatures, save two who escaped by means of a tree. As the form of a ship appears in this tradition, it is likely that the Mexican Noah and his wife rode safely over the deluge.

The **second age** was destroyed by wind. One man and one woman survived by concealing themselves in a hollow stone which was so heavy the wind couldn't blow it away.

In the **third age**, of fire, a terrible outburst of flame burned the entire world. Again, a Noah and wife were saved by seeking refuge in subterranean caverns where the terrible heat couldn't destroy them.

The **fourth age** is that in which sin—separation—destroys humanity, and according to the Maya, we are ending that period now.

Montezuma knew all of this, and from the same tradition he had learned that a **fifth age** was to come, a golden age in which the gods would return, or more correctly, turn with favor toward the nations of the Mesoamericans through their intermediary, the Feathered Serpent . . . Thus sayeth the Maya.

As we have retraced the Maya teachings, we have acquainted ourselves with the challenges this transition period offers. Now we search for solutions.

To help us free ourselves from the burdens of our age, according to Maya teachings, we have had from the date of Harmonic Convergence to this date in which to respond in a new way. The Maya say, "*to remember to remember is the way to easy living."*

Each day forms interlocking relational patterns with specific other days in the past or in the future, and allows players (in the game of Life) to travel forward or backward in time—or more precisely, allows the past and the future to come intuitively into the present. The present moment in the fourth dimension is the center of a spin that infinitely radiates clockwise and counterclockwise, creating the Eternal Now.

Jose Arguelles maintains there are five major steps in the advancement of humankind.
- The **first** revolution was the depiction of symbols on rocks
- The *second*, the invention of the alphabet
- The **third**, the invention of the printing press, enabling the production of books
- The **fourth** the computer technology revolution, creating instant communication
- Now, he maintains, this understanding is the **fifth**, as we realize . . . *WE ARE THE INFORMATION!*

The mindset of modern history is modulated by the 12:60 frequency—the frequency of materialism. In a system of materialism, we are reminded that: time is money; job loss causes fear; no one has enough.

The new frequency of 13:20 is to enable us to cut free of materialism and get on with our cosmic destiny. Our subconscious (lunar) memory will begin to remember our purpose, and the solar-tribe collective energy will begin to flow, to assist us to do our part.

Using our intuitive level of mind will assist us in staying in the here and now—awareness of the instant, not instant awareness. Each of us can only live in the present moment anyway, so it is an approach to assist us to re-learn about time and right use of the moment.

By breaking the code of the Maya culture with its many unusual calendars, Mayan teachers believe we are re-awakening to the galactic culture. The Maya have always taught that contact with the GALaxy was a part of human history

The message of Harmonic Convergence Quetzalcoatl tells us is:

"Everyone should wake up. The teaching is: Either all shall awaken with me, or if none awaken, I shall not awaken either. That's our deep spiritual nitty-gritty. The Galactic Federation is fourth dimensional intelligence and operates on trust—something that humans used to know about."

Learning to trust and support one another (Group Trust); so we can enter this frequency together is the work of the years of transition. Whatever is needed to create a way to free humanity from its old mindset is to happen—or so offer the Maya teachings.

To allow humanity to pass from materialism into galactic culture, to enter the kingdom of heaven, you have to become like a child—a child with a bright mind. We must own self-empowerment, self-divination, and self-discovery again. The message is: ***Tune in and take responsibility.***

After 5,000 years of the memory virus, the time of planetary renaissance and planetary reorganization is at hand. *"Our function is to flower,"* says Jose Arguelles. Now, you and I are going to allow these pieces of information to blossom in our lives as we free ourselves from the limitation of only the physical senses, and engage in a life of freedom—freedom to dream, to hope, to envision, and to trust.

Let us turn our attention to a series of thoughts and pictures as we begin our journey into galactic alignment:

As we read together the prayers of the aware ones of the past, we invoke their wisdom to be with us this day and in the days of the future.

Now a minute of silence, as we visualize the Light of the Solar Lord, the Great Lord Christ, to fill our mind. *Please, enter the SILENCE.*

A Meditation Adventure—Landing on a Planet

Close your eyes and become settled. I would ask you to assume that you and I are astronauts, not from Earth but from one of the many other thousands of inhabitable planets that exist in the GALaxy.

Long ago, we were launched from our planet. A robot set our course. After we escaped from orbit, we waited on our padded couches for the machines to take charge. We never heard the first whisper of gas as we fell asleep. The air crept hissing from the capsule and its heat drained into the ultimate cold of space. No decay could enter here. We lay in a tomb that would outlast any built on our planet—indeed, might outlast the planet itself. But it was more than a tomb, for its machines bide their time, and every hundred years a circuit opened and closed, counting the centuries.

So, we slept in our Cosmos, beyond reach of our Sun. In the world we had left, cities crumbled, mountains slid down, seas shrank, ice crawled and spread from the poles as our Sun cooled. We knew nothing of this, though probably we had foreseen it. Centuries lengthened into a millennium, and the millennium into aeons.

But at last, our ship remembers its commands given so long ago. It chooses a path toward a star that fits certain specifications programmed into its miniaturized brain. Out of millions of possible solar systems, it has happened to select the Sun that warms the planet Earth. It does not check speed until it is among the inner planets. Now it begins its search in the temperate zone where Mars and Venus and Earth circle. It presently recognizes a planet of the kind it seeks, and it veers into an orbit about the Earth.

For a while, the robot searches through its electronic memories and considers the situation. It makes the decision. If a robot could shrug its shoulder, it would do so. We *can always turn away and search elsewhere* if this planet doesn't fill the bill, it might be reminding us. It slowly begins to warm us, responding to signals from its external sensors. It wonders, "*Are you still with me?*"

You and I lie there for a while in a daze, knowing we can exist, not knowing who we are or whence we came. Then memory returns, and we stiffen with excitement. The curiosity which has sent us across the miles may soon be rewarded. Fully awakened now, we look down and study this new world which has been singled out for evaluation. Its size is correct, about the size of the home world we left. It has the necessary oceans, land masses and atmosphere. We circle closely, studying more detail. The chemical properties of the atmosphere coincide with those we know. Tests for carbon-based life forms are positive. Will it be warm enough for us, yet not too warm? The temperature spectrum is tolerable. Is the ground quaking? Apparently, not much.

The levels of activity are stable—relative gravity equal in force to our own. Cloud blankets obscure the land, but we make a dozen or more orbits. What we see looks good enough to justify an on-site inspection. We skim around in the lower altitudes. We get ready to release packs of guidance instruments, path-finding devices programmed to find deep water for soft splash-downs. We are looking for a large body of water near a flat, open plain, the higher the better. We prefer thin, clear atmosphere to minimize danger from infection, from gases—to enable our ship to soak up energy from strong solar radiation. Our commuter makes the final selection for the test drop.

We find a site within an area around a puma-shaped lake. If there, on that great bleak plain we finish our flight of fancy, we can land. If not, at the very least, we can drop seeds from the genetic code to become homo-sapiens. We can cruise off again and return at intervals to inspect the crops we have planted.

Take a breath. Remember yourself. Is this fantasy? Of course, but it is only the barest of possibilities that might have happened. In legends recorded centuries ago, the Indian people say, just such a peculiar event perhaps occurred at Lake Titicaca, and were told: "*do good to the whole world; give light that the humans may see, making them warm. Use my example, my children. Live for instruction, and benefit all those who live about you as beasts; and from this time, I will name you as lords. Go forth and bless them.*"

Let us remember that command. "*Go forth and be a blessing to all life.*" As you are ready, let's turn our attention outward.

Let us say as the Maya say:

"*In Lak' ech*" somewhat like "*in the Light of the Highest.*"

*   *   *

In conclusion: I have come to believe humanity will survive these difficult years and find its way to crack the cosmic egg becoming the long awaited possible human. For centuries, we have made efforts to overcome our prejudices and separations. These last few years have seen us make great strides: with each calamity I observe on television, I see wonderful human beings reaching out to assist others. Wealthy economists are beginning to sharing their bounty and roll-modeling sharing in ways little seen in the past. We will remember how to reach out to one another in more and more meaningful ways. I pray to God, we move rapidly into our potential.

LIST OF ILLUSTRATIONS

Reference list

Authors and books:
Jose Arguelles. *TIME & THE TECHNOSPHERE: Rochester, Vermont 05767, 2002: Bear and Company*

Jose Arguelles. The *Mayan Factor: Sante Fe, NM 87504: Bear and Company*

Alice Bailey, *A Treatise on the Seven Rays, pp.217-8: 1962 Treatise on White Magic, p. 379: 1951.* 120 Wall Street, 24th Floor, New York NY 10005, USA: Lucis Trust

Peter Balin. *The Flight of the Feathered Serpent: 1978: PO Box 21607 Detroit, Michigan 48221:Lotus Press*

Raymond Bernard. *Agharta: The Subterranean World:* 1960: P.O. Box 850,Pomeroy, WA 99347· Health Research Books

Carl Calleman, Paraphrased from The Crystal Skull Guardian Monthly News [md@ crystalskulls.com] and http://www.calleman.com/content/articles/risk_of_2012.htm

Col. James Churchward; *The Lost Continent of MU.* Albuquerque, NM: Brotherhood of Life 1987; *The Children of MU.* Albuquerque, NM: Brotherhood of Life 1988 Churchward calls his stories *"The Remains of Mu*

Andrew Collins. *Gateway to Atlantis*: 2000: 161 William Street, 16th Fl., NYC, NY 10038: pages 215-216: Avalon Publishing Group Incorporated

Willis George Emerson. The Smoky God: 1908: PO Box 301, Holicong, PA 18928-0301: Wildside Press

Admiral Richard E. Byrd. The Missing Diary of Admiral Richard E. Byrd: 1990: Inner Light Publications & Global Communications, International Society for a Complete Earth (ISCE) Danny L. Weiss P.O. Box 890 Felton, CA 05018

Raphael Girard's website, Spanish version of the *Popol Vuh* in 1948, English version1972

Carol E. Parrish Harra. *Esoteric Secrets of Sex, Passion and Love: 2011; and The New Dictionary of Spiritual Thought: 1994; 22 Summit Ridge Dr., Tahlequah, OK 74464: Sparrow Hawk Press*

Michael Harrington; *Touched by the Dragon's Breath.* Wilsonville, OR: Susan Creek Books 2005

Dr. Noel Huntley web-site: Beyond Duality www.users.globalnet.co.uk/~noelh

Hunbatz Men; Secrets of Mayan Science/Religion. Sante Fe, NM: Bear and Company,1990; *The 8 Calendars of the Maya.* Rochester, Vermont: Bear and Company, 1983

Ralph L. Roy's, *Books of Chilam Balam of Chumayel: Norman: University of OK Press 1967*

Dane Rudhyar, An Astrological Mandala

Torkom Saraydarian, *Cosmic Shocks, 1989: TSG Enterprises: PO Box 4273 West Hills, CA 91308*

Tony Shearer, *Beneath the Moon and Under the Sun,* 1975 Sun Publishing Company, P.O. BOX 5588 Santa Fe, New Mexico 87502-5588 *(and)The Lord of the Dawn,* 1995: Naturegraph Publishers, Incorporated, P.O. Box 1047 3543 Indian Creek Road Happy Camp, CA 96039

Rupert Sheldrake with Matthew Fox (page 4) *Physics of Angeles.* San Francisco, CA: HarperCollins & HarperSanFrancisco 1996

John Lloyd Stephens with artwork by Frederick Catherwood, *Incidents of Travel in Central America, Chiapas and Yucatan.* Mineola, NY: Dover Books 1969

Dennis Tedlock, Translated with commentary; *Popol Vuh,1985. NYC, NY: Simon and Schuster*

Sir Robert K. G. Temple in 1967. *The Sirius Mystery*

Sir Eric John Eric Thompson, *Maya History and Religion: Norman University Of Oklahoma Press 1970*

Jose Trigueirinho. *Calling Humanity,* chapters: Cosmic, Intraterrestial and Surface Races and Space Vessels pages 95-101)

Elizabeth Van Buren: *The Land of White Waters*, Bath, Avon BA 12PD, Ashgrove Press Limited: 1984

Erich Von Daniken watched the movie of

John White, *Pole Shift, The Meeting of Science and Spirit—Guidelines for a New Age* editor,

King Pacal Wikipedia www.wikipedia.com

Aluna Joy Yaxk'in alunajoy@kachina.net, The Prophecy of the Fifth World

Early in the 18th century (1701-1703), Father Francisco Ximenez discovered the *Popol Vuh* and translated it to Spanish.

World Age Rebirth!) www.13moons.com 2005 SkyTime 800-596-0835

The Structure of the Mayan Calendar insert here
http://www.oursacreduniverse.co.za/nayan.html

Hazel Henderson, Robert Theobald, Willis Harmon, the Green Party, and many others in spiritual activities. The World Healing Day, Earth Day and Earth Summit

Chris and Linda Lucz-Hatifeld, Blue Spectral Eagle and Blue Self-Existing Monkey . . . From Wacah Cahn Fall 1995